101
Cycling
Workouts

101
Cycling
Workouts

Improve Your Cycling Ability
While Adding Variety to your Training Program

David Ertl
USA CYCLING LEVEL 1 COACH

New York

101 Cycling Workouts
Improve Your Cycling Ability While Adding Variety to your Training Program

ISBN 978-1-60037-621-4

Library of Congress Control Number: 2009924310

MORGAN · JAMES
THE ENTREPRENEURIAL PUBLISHER

Morgan James Publishing, LLC
1225 Franklin Ave., STE 325
Garden City, NY 11530-1693
Toll Free 800-485-4943
www.MorganJamesPublishing.com

In an effort to support local communities, raise awareness and funds, Morgan James Publishing donates one percent of all book sales for the life of each book to Habitat for Humanity. Get involved today, visit **www.HelpHabitatForHumanity.org**.

Health Notice and Disclaimer

This book is intended to inform the reader about various cycling training workouts. **Many of the workouts outlined herein are strenuous in nature and should not be adopted without prior consultation with, and approval from, your health professional, or before you obtain proper instruction on technique from a qualified coach or personal trainer.** Cycling by nature is a dangerous activity and carries with it some inherent risks. Use of this information herein is at the sole choice and risk of the reader. The author is neither responsible nor liable for any harm or injury resulting from the use of the information described herein.

This book is dedicated to my Dad, who introduced me to the sport of cycling, which has become my lifelong passion.

CONTENTS

Preface xi

Chapter 1. How to Use This Book 1
    A. Explanation of workout formats 1
    B. Determining your workout training zones 2
    C. Modifying workouts to fit your ability 7
    D. Tips for putting workouts together to create a structured
    training plan 8

Chapter 2. Recovery Workouts 11

Chapter 3. Endurance Workouts 15

Chapter 4. Tempo Workouts 21

Chapter 5. Threshold Workouts 27

Chapter 6. Anaerobic Workouts 45

Chapter 7. Sprint and Power Workouts 65

Chapter 8. Leg Strength Workouts 73

Chapter 9. Leg Speed Workouts 103

Chapter 10. Cross-Training Workouts 111

Chapter 11. Testing Workouts 127

Chapter 12. Races as Workouts 137

Chapter 13. Recovery Exercises 145

Chapter 14. Workout 101: The Joy Ride! 151

Preface

This book contains 101 training workouts for road cyclists. It is intended to provide you with a menu of many possible rides and workout options as you plan your training rides and program. *There is no reason to be bored* or reach a plateau in your training if you use even half of these workouts. Workouts are grouped according to the type of physiological system trained, so you can easily find workouts for the given objective of the day. Remember, *every ride or workout should have a purpose*: to improve some aspect of your cycling fitness. Each chapter offers multiple workouts to target each particular physiological system. This book can also serve as a companion to training plans and other books that offer a training outline but don't provide specific workouts or a wide enough variety of workouts. So try a variety of workouts offered in this book. Just remember to ask your physician before beginning a strenuous exercise program. You won't like all of these workouts, but you will find some that become favorites. The important thing to remember is to continue to stress your body in new and different ways. That's how you will improve, by continually changing up your routine and throwing different workouts at your body. The workouts contained within this book can do that for you.

If you are interested in obtaining training plans using these workouts, or if you are interested in personal coaching, visit www.CyclesportCoaching.com for more information.

Coach David Ertl

Chapter 1
How to Use This Book

A. Explanation of workout formats

Most of the workouts in this book are structured in a similar format.

Purpose of Workout: Explains the particular physiological aspect of cycling that the workout is intended to improve and contains information on when to use it in a training program along with other benefits of the workout.

Course Description: Explains the type of route best suited for the given ride, such as level, hilly, or into a headwind. It also identifies those workouts that are better done on an indoor trainer to provide a controlled environment. Many of these cycling workouts can be done either outdoors or on a trainer, but there are some, due to their nature, that can only be done one way or the other and these are identified.

Workout Description: Describes the workout in enough detail to allow you to understand how to do the workout. It discusses the warm-up, the main body of the workout, number of intervals if applicable, workout duration, and cool down.

Modifications: Lists other ways in which the workout can be done, or adaptations to it. Many, but not all, of the workouts offer such modifications.

Some of the workouts, particularly those involving strength training in the gym, have different categories:

Equipment: When necessary, describes supplemental equipment that is required or helpful to conduct the workout, such as specific weight equipment.

Exercise Description: Contains specific instructions on how to do an exercise and involves detailed explanation where proper technique is important, such as when doing a squat.

B. Determining your workout training zones

Training Zones: Training zones are used to prescribe the intensity at which you should do these workouts. In order to get the desired benefits from these workouts, you need to make sure you are doing them at the proper effort level to elicit the desired physiological responses. The cardiovascular system is involved in circulating blood, which carries essential nutrients and oxygen to the working muscles. The type of metabolic response one experiences is determined by the percentage of capacity at which one is exercising. These effort levels are based on the percentage of your Anaerobic Threshold (AT) using a heart rate monitor or Threshold Power (TP) using a power meter. Heart rate and power zones are listed in these workouts, which target the physiological system most impacted by the workout. For example, zone 2 workouts are at a heart rate that is fairly low, and this emphasizes those metabolic systems important for low-intensity endurance workouts. For determination of your zones, percentage of AT, not percentage of maximum heart rate (MHR), will be used. The main reason for this is because it's difficult and risky to test one's maximum heart rate, whereas it is possible to estimate your AT quite accurately and safely. If you have a power meter, there are power zones similar to heart rate zones, and those are described below, as is the method for determining your own zones.

There are several versions of zones used by coaches; the system used in this book has 6 levels:

Zone 1 = Recovery
Zone 2 = Endurance
Zone 3 = Tempo
Zone 4 = Threshold
Zone 5 = Anaerobic
Zone 6 = Maximal Effort

Lactate Threshold (LT) or Anaerobic Threshold (AT): Lactate or anaerobic threshold is the effort level at which you begin to accumulate lactic acid in your muscles; anaerobic threshold indicates the heart rate at which anaerobic energy production surpasses your aerobic energy production. It is also the rate at which your effort is no longer sustainable for long periods of time (e.g., > 1 hour). AT generally occurs at 85–92% of MHR. See the section below to determine your heart rate zones.

Heart Rate Zones:

> **Zone 1** = Recovery (<71% of AT) – uses the aerobic system

> **Zone 2** = Endurance (72–81% of AT) – uses the aerobic system

> **Zone 3** = Tempo Pace (82–91% of AT) – uses mainly the aerobic system

> **Zone 4** = Threshold Pace (92–102% of AT) – uses mainly the aerobic system with some of the anaerobic system

> **Zone 5** = Anaerobic Pace (103–110% of AT) – uses the anaerobic system to a large degree in addition to the aerobic system

> **Zone 6** = Maximum Aerobic Capacity (too short to record HR but greater than 105% of AT) – uses the anaerobic and creatine phosphate systems

Threshold Power (TP): TP is the sustainable power output you can produce for up to an hour. This generally corresponds closely to your anaerobic threshold level. See the section below to determine your power zones.

Power Zones:

> **Zone 1** = Recovery (<55% of TP) – uses the aerobic system

> **Zone 2** = Endurance (56–75% of TP) – uses the aerobic system

> **Zone 3** = Tempo Pace (76–90% of TP) – uses mainly the aerobic system

Zone 4 = Threshold Pace (91–105% of TP) – uses mainly the aerobic system with some of the anaerobic system

Zone 5 = Anaerobic Pace (106–120% of TP) – uses the anaerobic system to a large degree in addition to the aerobic system

Zone 6 = Maximum Aerobic Capacity (V02 Max) (>120% of TP) – uses the anaerobic and creatine phosphate systems

<u>Determining Your AT and TP:</u> Because AT and TP are based on the maximum sustainable pace you can maintain for up to an hour, it's possible to estimate this heart rate or power from a shorter time trial effort, such as a 20-minute time trial. Find a road that is relatively level and free of traffic and intersections. If you can't find a stretch of road that allows you to ride this long, find a road that's about 5 miles and do an "out-and-back" course to get your 20-minute test done. Alternately, you can do this on an indoor trainer. In some ways, an indoor trainer gives you a more repeatable result as you don't have the weather and traffic variables. Warm up thoroughly and then begin the 20-minute time trial. Ride as hard as you can at a pace you can maintain for the full 20 minutes. There is a fine line between going out too fast and not pushing yourself hard enough. You may need to do a few of these before you figure out your true sustainable pace. Record your heart rate and/or power towards the end of the 20 minutes. Do not accelerate or sprint at the end. What you are after is your sustainable, steady-state heart rate or power. If you have a computer that allows you, take the average heart rate or power for the last 10 minutes of the effort.

The pace you can maintain for 20 minutes is slightly faster than the pace you can maintain for an hour. So take your heart rate or power from this 20-minute test and multiply by 0.95 to arrive at your sustainable pace, which is your estimated Anaerobic Threshold (AT) or Threshold Power (PT). Use this value to estimate your own zones, and you will be able to know your own heart rate or power zones that are described in the Workout Description of each workout.

Use the chart below to identify your zones based on the AT and TP values obtained from your test.

Heart Rate–Based Training Zones (in Beats per Minute)

AT Heart Rate (Beat/Min)	Recovery Zone 1	Endurance Zone 2	Tempo Zone 3	Threshold Zone 4	Anaerobic Zone 5	Max Effort Zone 6
130	<94	94–107	108–120	121–134	135–143	>143
135	<97	97–111	112–124	125–139	140–149	>149
140	<101	101–115	116–129	130–144	145–154	>154
145	<104	104–119	120–133	134–149	150–160	>160
150	<108	108–123	124–138	139–155	156–165	>165
155	<112	112–127	128–143	144–160	161–171	>171
160	<115	115–131	132–147	148–165	166–176	>176
165	<119	119–135	136–152	153–170	171–182	>182
170	<122	122–139	140–156	157–175	176–187	>187
175	<126	127–144	145–161	162–180	181–193	>193
180	<130	130–148	149–166	167–185	186–198	>198
185	<133	133–152	153–170	171–191	192–204	>204
190	<137	137–156	157–175	176–196	197–209	>209
195	<140	140–160	161–179	180–201	202–215	>215

Power Training Zones (in Watts)

Threshold Power (Watts)	Recovery Zone 1	Endurance Zone 2	Tempo Zone 3	Threshold Zone 4	Anaerobic Zone 5	Max Effort Zone 6
200	<110	110–150	151–182	183–212	213–240	>240
210	<116	116–158	159–191	192–223	224–252	>252
220	<121	121–165	166–200	201–233	234–264	>264
230	<127	127–173	174–209	210–244	245–276	>276
240	<132	132–180	181–218	219–254	255–288	>288
250	<138	138–188	189–228	229–265	266–300	>300
260	<143	143–195	196–237	238–276	277–312	>312
270	<149	149–203	204–246	247–286	287–324	>324
280	<154	154–210	211–255	256–297	298–336	>336
290	<160	160–218	219–264	265–307	308–348	>348
300	<165	165–225	226–273	274–318	319–360	>360
310	<171	171–233	234–282	283–329	330–372	>372
320	<176	176–240	241–291	292–339	340–384	>384
330	<182	182–248	249–300	301–350	351–396	>396

C. Modifying workouts to fit your ability

The workouts in this book are targeted at an average fit cyclist. Cyclists who are just beginning a training program will find many of these workouts too difficult to complete as designed. Very fit competitors may not find them challenging enough. Here are some suggestions for modifying these workouts to fit your ability.

If you find these workouts too challenging, or you don't have enough time to complete the entire workout, you may reduce the length of the workout or the number of intervals when provided. For example, in workout 26, the 6-minute uphill intervals, the Workout Description says to do 4 of these intervals. If you are just starting this type of training, you may only be able to complete 2 of these at the prescribed intensity. That's okay. Next time try to add another interval.

If you find these intervals easy to accomplish, you can add additional intervals to the workout. If you find these workouts too easy in general, your threshold may be estimated too low and you may want to repeat the test and get a new estimate on your threshold level.

In any case, don't increase or decrease the intensity above or below the zone prescribed. To work the intended system (aerobic, anaerobic, power), you need to work in the zone given; otherwise, you turn the workout into a different workout targeting a different system. Some latitude in the heart rate and power zones is given so you can work within those ranges, either higher or lower depending on your situation. But if you find yourself dropping from zone 5 to zone 4 in anaerobic intervals, back off on the number of intervals rather than reducing the intensity. Also, don't increase or decrease the length of the prescribed intervals. That changes the physiological system being targeted. This book has many options for aerobic and anaerobic intervals. If you find you can't do all of the 2-minute intervals in workout 37, try doing 1-minute intervals in workout 36 first. Both of these are short and work similar systems. Again, don't reduce your level of effort on these just to finish the interval. If you can only complete 1.5 minutes instead of 2 minutes, it's better to do a good minute and a half than to compromise the quality of the workout just to do the prescribed length of the intervals. Always think quality over quantity.

On zone 2 endurance rides and zone 3 tempo rides, you can increase or decrease the distance to fit your schedule and ability. However, for the most benefit, you need to do these for at least an hour and a half per workout.

D. Tips for putting workouts together to create a structured training plan

This book is primarily intended to give you new ideas for training using a wide variety of workouts to improve your cycling. The way in which you put these workouts together is very important as well. It doesn't matter what workout you do if you only work out once every 2 weeks. You just won't see improvement. Likewise, if you train hard every day, you will become chronically fatigued and will not be able to put in quality efforts after 2 to 3 days, and you will plateau and likely burn out. You need a variety of different types of workouts put together in a systematic manner to make the most of your training time, and you should combine these with recovery days. This is where a coach comes in. A coach works with you using your abilities and goals to put together a combination of workouts and intermixes these with appropriate recovery workouts. While this chapter in no way intends to replace a coach, it can give you some pointers on how to design your own program using these workouts.

Types of workouts: For an all-around cycling fitness or competitive road racing program, you should do workouts from every chapter, from endurance through power and strength workouts. If you are more of a time trialist or triathlete, you should focus on endurance, tempo, threshold, and strength workouts. If you are a recreational cyclist and want to improve your touring ability, concentrate on endurance, tempo, and strength workouts.

Frequency of workouts: Plan your week by deciding how many workouts you can do. This is a combination of your ability, goals, age, and time available. If you are young and want to be a top competitor, you should do 4 hard workouts each week. If you are a recreational cyclist and just want to stay fit, maybe 2 is enough. As people get older, their recovery time increases, and they need to take more recovery days and do fewer hard workouts each week. You may only be able to do 3 hard workouts a week whereas you used to do 4. If that is the case, rest and recover well between hard days and then give it your all when you do have a hard workout to get the most out of those efforts. Once you know how many hard workouts you plan to do, set up your week so that you have no more than 2 hard workouts on back-to-back days. For example, if you want to do 4 hard workouts in a given week, you may plan those for Tuesday, Thursday, Saturday, and Sunday. This spreads them out during the week and gives you a day between workouts except for Saturday and Sunday. If you only plan to do 2, you might do your hardest workouts on Tuesday and Saturday to give yourself maximum time between workouts to recover.

Putting together an annual cycle of workouts: Your training should vary throughout the year. If you live in a climate where there are 4 seasons, this helps provide a natural cycle to your training. Here's a simplified example of how you might think about setting up an annual plan. During the winter, or off-season, you can do 2 strength workouts with perhaps only 1 zone 4 workout and 1 or 2 longer zone 2 rides per week. As spring arrives, build your aerobic base back up, concentrating on zone 2 and 3 rides with 1 strength and 1 threshold (zone 4) workout per week. As your main riding season starts, begin adding in a zone 5 anaerobic and then zone 6 power workout if appropriate and back off on the endurance rides. Throughout the year, continue to do recovery and leg speed workouts on easy days.

For examples of annual training plans, see www.CyclesportCoaching.com for plans focusing on recreational cyclists, competitive racers, and time trialists/triathletes to get ideas on how to put a structured plan together.

Chapter 2
Recovery Workouts

It may seem odd to start off this book with recovery workouts, but the workouts in this book are listed in order by level of difficulty from easier to more strenuous, and recovery workouts are the easiest of workouts. It's also good to put them up front to remind cyclists that recovery is just as important as working out. If you ride hard all the time but never rest to allow your body and mind to recover, eventually you will plateau and become stale, and you will not get the improvements you want. These recovery workouts are designed to provide your legs with the rest they need and to also help them recover more quickly than doing nothing, a concept called "active recovery." These workouts get your leg muscles and joints moving to help flush away metabolic waste products, loosen up tight and sore muscles, and get your blood circulating to help speed recovery. These workouts will also give your head a mental break from harder training. Keep in mind, training breaks your body down; it's the recovery that builds it back up stronger! Don't underestimate the power and importance of these easy workouts. Recovery is a key element for improvement. These recovery workouts should be done 2 to 3 times per week.

Workout 1: Recovery Spin

Purpose of Workout: This is an active recovery ride to loosen up stiff, sore legs and to circulate blood to flush out waste products. Easy riding is a form of muscle massage. This is meant to be done on days following hard workouts to speed recovery or on days leading up to a big ride or race during a taper. Being a recovery workout, this is meant to rest all systems and allow their recovery. This workout should not add to fatigue.

Course Description: This workout should be done on a fairly level road, or if that isn't possible, spin a low gear on the uphills. This can also be done on an indoor trainer with no or light resistance and is great to do on rollers with no resistance. It can also be done on a mountain bike on the road or trails in a low gear.

Workout Description: This entire ride should be ridden in a low gear with a fairly high cadence (85–95 RPM). If hills are encountered, downshift so you can spin up them. It should feel as though there is no pressure on the legs. Total workout length: 30–45 minutes.

Modification: If legs are feeling good, you can throw in a few low-gear sprints of 15–20 seconds, spinning up to 120 RPM.

Workout 2: Race Prep Tune-Up

Purpose of Workout: To prepare you mentally and physically for a race or big ride the following day. This provides both active recovery and some easy efforts to keep your systems tuned up and ready to go. This workout is meant to be a recovery-type ride for the legs and a few efforts to open up the lungs and cardiovascular system. It's also meant to help prepare the mind for the upcoming race or ride.

Course Description: This workout should be done on a fairly level road, or if that isn't possible, spin a low gear on the uphills. This can also be done on a trainer with light resistance. This ride should be done on the same bike that is to be used for the race, to ensure it's in perfect working order.

Workout Description: This entire ride should be ridden in a low gear with a fairly high cadence (85–95 RPM). If hills are encountered, gear down so you can spin up them. It should feel as though there is no pressure on the legs. Every 5 minutes or so, throw in an interval of 30 seconds, using a low gear. This should be enough of an effort to increase the heart rate up to zone 4–5 briefly. Total workout length: 30–45 minutes.

Modifications: If legs are feeling fresh, you can use a somewhat higher gear during the intervals to imitate a sprint.

Workout 3: Day Off

Purpose of Workout: A day off may not seem like a "workout," but it is an important part of training and improving. This is a passive recovery day during which you don't work out and you give your body and mind a complete rest. It may be out of necessity due to a hectic schedule or travel, or it may be intentional to recharge your batteries. Taking one day completely off per week is a good idea, and you should not feel guilty at all about it. Think of it as part of your training, which it is.

Course Description: None.

Workout Description: Don't ride or work out but try to get a good night's sleep, eat healthfully, and stay hydrated. You may choose to massage your legs. Total workout length: 0 minutes.

Modifications: You can go for a walk or do something other than cycling as long as it is not intense exercise and you aren't on your feet a long time. Resist the temptation to go for a ride if your plan has a scheduled day off. Take the day off and come back tomorrow even more eager to train.

Chapter 3
Endurance Workouts

Endurance workouts are the foundation of any cycling fitness program. Regardless of the type of riding you do, developing base conditioning with endurance is essential. This should seem obvious as road cycling is an endurance sport. Endurance creates the aerobic base upon which to build with more advanced workouts. Think of endurance training as your foundation. Without the ability to sit on your bike, spinning your legs for hours, there is no way you are going to be able to ride faster or stronger for any distance. Endurance training accomplishes a number of physiological changes, most notably an increase in aerobic capacity, adaptation of cellular and blood chemistries to improve your metabolic efficiency, increase in leg strength, and increased capillaries in the leg muscles, and it trains your body to sit and spin on a bike for hours on end. Endurance rides are typically done throughout the year but are emphasized at the beginning of the season to build a solid foundation for more strenuous training to follow during the season.

Workout 4: LSD Ride

Purpose of Workout: This is a <u>L</u>ong <u>S</u>teady <u>D</u>istance ride. Some use LSD to mean <u>L</u>ong <u>S</u>LOW <u>D</u>istance (and others think of something else altogether!). But I prefer to use the term Long STEADY Distance. Its purpose is to get the body used to sitting in the saddle for long periods of time, to adapt your metabolism to be efficient and burn fat, and to improve your aerobic fitness.

Course Description: Find a route that allows you to go the distance required to get in the length of ride you want. It can either be a loop or an out-and-back route. For variety, the course can have some hills of varying difficultly. Make sure you take enough food and water or have places identified on the route to stop and refuel and get water.

Workout Description: This ride should be ridden in zone 2 for the most part, but on hills your heart rate will move into zone 3 and possibly into zone 4 for brief periods. The bulk of the ride should be at a comfortable but steady pace. Avoid letting it lull you into a recovery zone 1 pace. An endurance ride should be at least 90 minutes to gain the desired benefits. Total workout length: 90 minutes to 4 hours.

Modification: You can do it with others to keep you company but be careful that it doesn't become a tempo or faster paced ride.

Workout 5: Hilly Endurance Ride

Purpose of Workout: This ride has all the benefits of the LSD ride (Workout 4) but also incorporates more hills, and the idea is to work hard on the hills. Hills throw in random intervals to get your heart rate up and force you to use more leg muscles than on a flat, steady endurance ride.

Course Description: Find a route that provides plenty of hills of varying length and difficulty. It can either be a loop or an out-and-back route. Make sure you take enough food and water or have places identified on the route to stop and refuel and get water.

Workout Description: This ride should be ridden in zone 2 for the most part. As you approach hills, increase your effort, and your heart rate will move into zones 3 and 4 during the hill climbs, either sitting on the saddle or standing, or a combination of both. Resume a zone 2 pace once you have reached the top of the hill. An endurance ride should be at least 90 minutes to gain the desired benefits. Total workout length: 90 minutes to 4 hours.

Modifications: You can do it with others to keep you company but be careful that it doesn't become a tempo or faster paced ride.

Workout 6: Endurance Ride with 5-Minute Intervals

Purpose of Workout: This is primarily an endurance ride but has some threshold intervals thrown in to increase the effort and pace. These intervals will cause you to fatigue faster than riding steadily at an endurance pace. This works aerobic fitness both in terms of endurance and in terms of sustaining a higher pace during a long ride.

Course Description: Find a route that allows you to go the distance required to get in the length of ride you want. It can either be a loop or an out-and-back route. The course should be level for the most part. If you have nothing but hills near you, try to do the intervals during level areas of the course or on steady climbs.

Workout Description: After a 15–20-minute warm-up, start your first 5-minute interval at your zone 4 or threshold pace. After the interval, resume a zone 2 pace for the next 15 minutes. Repeat the 5-minute intervals every 20 minutes or so, depending on the terrain, for the duration of the ride. This ride should be ridden in zone 2 for the most part, but your heart rate will move into zones 3 and 4 during the intervals. Your last 5-minute interval should be several miles from home to allow for a cool down at the end of the ride. An endurance ride should be at least 90 minutes to gain the desired benefits. Total workout length: 90 minutes to 4 hours.

Modifications: You can also do these with 10-minute intervals instead of 5-minute intervals. You can do it with others to keep you company but try to find people who are of somewhat equal ability and explain to them what you are doing or they may think you don't like them because you will be accelerating away from them every 15 minutes.

Workout 7: Endurance Ride with a Fast Push at the End

Purpose of Workout: This is an endurance ride, but instead of finishing at the same speed as (or slower than) the entire ride, this one finishes with a faster push at the end of the ride, when you are most tired. This will help train you to continue to push hard right through to the end of a long ride, making you better able to keep up your pace on a long ride or preparing you for the fast finish of a race.

Course Description: Find a route that allows you to go the distance required to get in the length of ride you want. It can either be a loop or an out-and-back route. It can be hilly or level.

Workout Description: This ride should be ridden in zone 2 for the most part, but on hills your heart rate will move into zone 3 and possibly into zone 4 for brief periods. The bulk of the ride should be at a comfortable but steady pace. About 30 minutes from the end of your ride, increase your pace. You should get into zone 3–4 for this portion of the ride. Continue to push this pace for 20 minutes, then back off and spin in for the final 10 minutes of the ride as a cool down. Total workout length: 90 minutes to 4 hours.

Modification: Throw in a sprint at the end of the final 20-minute push to simulate the end of a road race.

Chapter 4
Tempo Workouts

Tempo pace is faster than endurance pace but slower than threshold pace. This pace requires some concentration to maintain as it is getting into the range where it begins to become slightly harder and is more work to maintain than endurance pace. But the efforts are not "hard" and shouldn't be painful; they just require concentration. Tempo workouts are good to build speed for fairly long distances. It's often the pace that occurs when riding with others. Cyclists tend to push the pace when riding with others. It's good to incorporate some tempo rides in with endurance rides as your base fitness improves. This will stimulate your body to get used to a faster pace and avoid getting into a rut of zone 2 training. However, because zone 3 is harder than zone 2, you need to be careful of not doing too many zone 3 rides each week as they can fatigue you and prevent you from getting in quality workouts on other days. One tempo workout per week should be enough if you are doing other workouts.

Workout 8: Tempo Endurance Ride

Purpose of Workout: This is an endurance ride but is ridden at a faster pace than endurance pace. This pace shouldn't be uncomfortable but also should require some focus to keep the pace up. This ride will increase your ability to ride long endurance rides more comfortably and to ride them at a faster pace.

Course Description: Find a route that allows you to go the distance required to get in the length of ride you want. It can either be a loop or an out-and-back route. For variety, you can ride some hills of varying difficultly.

Workout Description: Following a 15-minute warm-up in zone 2, increase the pace to low zone 3 for the bulk of the ride. On hills, your heart rate may move into zone 4 for brief periods. Avoid letting yourself drift back into an endurance zone 2 pace. This will require constant attention to your pace. A tempo endurance ride should be at least 90 minutes in duration. Total workout length: 90 minutes to 3 hours.

Modifications: These are great rides to do with others as long as you avoid the temptation of going too hard and turning it into a threshold ride, which is the tendency when riding with others.

Workout 9: Tempo Ride

Purpose of Workout: This is a ride ridden at tempo (zone 3) pace but is shorter than an endurance ride. This pace shouldn't be uncomfortable but also should require constant focus to keep the pace up. This ride will increase your ability to ride long endurance rides more comfortably and to cruise along at a faster pace.

Course Description: Find a route that allows you to go the distance required to get in the length of ride you want. It can either be a loop or an out-and-back route. For variety, it can have some hills of varying difficultly. These are good rides to do when you don't have a lot of time. They should be done after an aerobic endurance base has been developed.

Workout Description: Following a 15-minute warm-up in zone 2, increase the pace to mid to high zone 3 for the remainder of the ride. On hills, your heart rate may move into zone 4 for brief periods. Avoid letting yourself drift back into an endurance zone 2 pace. This will require constant attention to your pace. A tempo ride should be no more than 90 minutes in duration. Total workout length: 45–90 minutes.

Modifications: These are great rides to do with others as you will tend to keep each other going.

Workout 10: Group Rides

Purpose of Workout: Group rides are a fun way to get in a hard workout. Rides with others tend to be faster than any rides you would do alone (no one wants to appear slow when riding with his or her peers). Therefore, group rides are a good way to get in a tempo ride. This ride is ridden at tempo (zone 3) pace for the most part, but due to the fact that you are riding with others, paces may differ throughout the ride, which is okay. This ride will increase your ability to ride long endurance rides more comfortably and to cruise along at a fast pace. It will also give you experience riding in close proximity to other riders to develop your bike-handling skills. The big watch-out with group rides is they tend to become hammer fests, where the pace continues to accelerate until everyone is anaerobic.

Course Description: Find a route that allows you to go the distance required to get in the length of ride you want. It can either be a loop or an out-and-back route. The course will likely be determined by the group with which you are riding. This ride should be done after an aerobic endurance base has been developed.

Workout Description: The group should warm up at the beginning of the ride. The group pace will largely be out of your control, but you can help push the pace if you need to. It's difficult to slow a group down, though, if it goes faster than you want. Try to stay with the group, but if you are intent on keeping your pace in zone 3 and their pace is pushing you into zone 4 (or, yikes, higher), then you will have to make a decision as to whether you can and want to continue riding with the group or drop off and maintain your own pace. There's nothing wrong with going into zone 4, just realize this is a different workout (a threshold workout). Total workout length: 45 minutes to 2 hours.

Modifications: It's okay to throw in sprints to stop signs or city limit signs, as long as they are short and playful.

Workout 11: Tempo Intervals

Purpose of Workout: This is a ride that alternates endurance and tempo pace throughout the ride. It forces you to be able to repeatedly increase the pace throughout the ride. This is helpful in getting you used to riding faster than your normal endurance pace and helps you to maintain a faster pace for longer periods.

Course Description: Find a route that allows you to go the distance required to get in the length of ride you want. It can either be a loop or an out-and-back route. It's better to have a level course as hills will interrupt your ability to control your pace.

Workout Description: After a 15-minute warm-up at zone 2 pace, increase pace to zone 3 and hold for 5 to 10 minutes. Then back down to zone 2 for an equal period of time. Repeat this sequence for the duration of the ride. Cool down at the end of the ride in zone 1–2 for 10 minutes. Total workout length: 45 minutes to 3 hours.

Modifications: This is also a good workout to do on an indoor trainer to help break the monotony of slogging along at the same mind-numbing pace on longer indoor rides.

Chapter 5
Threshold Workouts

Threshold workouts are a mainstay of cycling training if you wish to maintain and improve your aerobic capacity. Your aerobic threshold is the amount of effort you can maintain for at least an hour. It is right at the boundary between where you can supply ample oxygen to your muscles and where you begin to run short of oxygen and go anaerobic. Aerobic fitness will enable you to be a better rider as you will be able to ride faster before you enter your anaerobic zones, which are very expensive metabolically and will tire you out quickly. The larger your aerobic engine is, the more speed and power you can produce and maintain for long periods of time. Threshold workouts are hard and require a lot of concentration. You should do these almost year-round to maintain your aerobic fitness, and they can be done up to twice per week.

Workout 12: 5-Minute Intervals

Purpose of Workout: This workout trains you to maintain your sustainable time trial or threshold pace for 5 minutes at a time. This is a good workout to do when you are trying to work up to holding your time trial pace for longer periods but can't yet maintain 10 or 20 minutes at a time.

Course Description: Threshold workouts are best done on level or slightly rolling terrain. It's more difficult to maintain your targeted effort on hills, both going up and coming down. Choose either an out-and-back course or a large loop. Try to avoid roads with lots of intersections, stop signs, stoplights, and traffic as these will interfere with your ability to ride for 5 minutes at a time without interruption.

Workout Description: Following a 15-minute warm-up in zone 2, increase the pace to zone 4 and hold this pace for 5 minutes. Then back down to zone 1–2 for 5 minutes and repeat. Cool down for 10 minutes at the end. Initially you may only be able to do 3 or 4 intervals. Try to work up to 8 to 10 of these, or move on to the 10-, 15-, or 20-minute intervals. Avoid going out too fast on your first interval. Total workout length: 1 to 2 hours, depending on the number of intervals.

Modifications: These can also be done on the indoor trainer, even in the summer, if you don't have suitable roads. The trainer is actually more conducive to doing controlled intervals.

Workout 13: 10-Minute Intervals

Purpose of Workout: This workout trains you to maintain your sustainable time trial or threshold pace for 10 minutes at a time. This is a good workout to do when you are trying to work up to holding your time trial pace for longer periods but can't yet maintain 20–30 minutes at a time.

Course Description: Threshold workouts are best done on level or slightly rolling terrain. It's more difficult to maintain your targeted effort on hills. Choose either an out-and-back course or a large loop. Try to avoid roads with lots of intersections, stop signs, stoplights, and traffic as these will interfere with your ability to ride for 10 minutes at a time without interruption.

Workout Description: Following a 15-minute warm-up in zone 2, increase the pace to zone 4 and hold this pace for 10 minutes. Then back down to zone 1–2 for 10 minutes and repeat this sequence. Cool down for 10 minutes at the end. Initially you may only be able to do a couple of these intervals. Try to work up to 5 of these and then move on to the 15- or 20-minute intervals. Avoid going out too fast on your first interval; rather, try to pick a pace and hold it steadily all the way through all intervals. Total workout length: 1 to 2 hours, depending on the number of intervals.

Modifications: These can also be done on the indoor trainer, even in the summer, if you don't have suitable roads. The trainer is actually more conducive to doing controlled intervals.

Workout 14: 15-Minute Intervals

Purpose of Workout: This workout trains you to maintain your sustainable time trial or threshold pace for 15 minutes at a time. This is a good workout to do when you are building up for a time trial of 15 minutes or longer.

Course Description: Threshold workouts are best done on level or slightly rolling terrain. It's more difficult to maintain your targeted effort on hills. Choose either an out-and-back course or a large loop. Try to avoid roads with lots of intersections, stop signs, stoplights, and traffic as these will interfere with your ability to ride for 15 minutes at a time without interruption.

Workout Description: Following a 15-minute warm-up in zone 2, increase the pace to low zone 4 and hold this pace for 15 minutes. Then back down to zone 1–2 for 10 minutes and repeat a second time. Cool down for 10 minutes at the end. Initially you may only be able to do 1 interval. Try to work up to 4 of these if your goal is a 40K time trial, or move up to 20-minute intervals. Avoid going out too fast on the first interval; rather, try to maintain a steady pace throughout. Total workout length: 1 to 2 hours, depending on the number of intervals.

Modifications: These can also be done on the indoor trainer, even in the summer, if you don't have suitable roads. The trainer is actually more conducive to doing controlled intervals.

Workout 15: 20-Minute Intervals

Purpose of Workout: This workout trains you to maintain your sustainable time trial or threshold pace for 20 minutes at a time. This is a good workout to do when you are building up for a time trial of 20 minutes or longer.

Course Description: Threshold workouts are best done on level or slightly rolling terrain. It's more difficult to maintain your targeted effort on hills. Choose either an out-and-back course or a large loop. Try to avoid roads with lots of intersections, stop signs, stoplights, and traffic as these will interfere with your ability to ride for 20 minutes at a time without too much interruption.

Workout Description: Following a 15-minute warm-up in zone 2, increase the pace to low zone 4 and hold this pace for 20 minutes. Then back down to zone 1–2 for 10 minutes and repeat a second time. Cool down for 10 minutes at the end. Initially you may only be able to do 1 interval. Try to work up to 3 of these if your goal is a 40K time trial. Avoid going out too fast on the first interval. Total workout length: 1 to 2 hours, depending on the number of intervals.

Modifications: These can also be done on the indoor trainer, even in the summer, if you don't have suitable roads. The trainer is actually more conducive to doing controlled intervals.

Workout 16: 30-Minute Time Trial

Purpose of Workout: This workout trains you to ride a time trial. Your objective is to hold your sustainable zone 4 pace for the duration of this ride. Part of the training is learning to pace yourself to ride a steady and sustainable pace for the duration of the time trial. It is good training for an actual time trial and is also a good test to do periodically to track your progress.

Course Description: Threshold workouts are best done on level or slightly rolling terrain. It's more difficult to maintain your targeted effort on hills. Choose either an out-and-back course or a loop that can be ridden multiple times to allow you to ride for 30 minutes. Try to avoid roads with lots of intersections, stop signs, stoplights, and traffic as these will interfere with your ability to ride for 30 minutes at a time without unnecessary interruption.

Workout Description: Following a good 15-minute warm-up in zone 2, increase the pace to zone 4 and hold this pace for 30 minutes. Cool down for 15 minutes at the end. Avoid going out too fast at the beginning, a very common error. Use a heart rate monitor or power meter to judge your effort. If possible, record your speed and heart rate/power during this ride and compare it to other 30-minute time trials to determine if you are able to ride faster at a similar heart rate and/or power. Note that your speed will be a function not only of your fitness but also of the weather conditions, so don't base your appraisal of your ride simply on speed, although that's one indicator. Total workout length: 1 hour.

Modifications: This workout can also be done on the indoor trainer, even in the summer, if you don't have suitable roads. The trainer is actually more conducive to comparing performances.

Workout 17: 60-Minute Time Trial

Purpose of Workout: This workout trains you to ride a 40K time trial. Your objective is to hold your sustainable zone 4 pace for the duration of this ride. Part of this training is learning to pace yourself to ride a steady and sustainable pace for the duration of the time trial. It is good training for an actual time trial and is also a good test to do periodically to track your progress. However, this is a difficult workout and should not be done very often, especially if you are competing in a lot of time trials.

Course Description: Threshold workouts are best done on level or slightly rolling terrain. It's more difficult to maintain your targeted effort on hilly courses. Choose either an out-and-back course or a loop that can be ridden multiple times to be able to ride for the full 60 minutes. Try to avoid roads with lots of intersections, stop signs, stoplights, and traffic as these will interfere with your ability to ride for 60 minutes at a time without interruption.

Workout Description: Following a good 15-minute warm-up in zone 2, increase the pace to zone 4 and hold this pace for 60 minutes. Cool down for 10 minutes at the end. Avoid going out too fast at the beginning, which is a very common error. Use a heart rate monitor or power meter to judge your effort if you can. If possible, record your speed and heart rate and/or power during this ride and compare it to other 60-minute time trials to determine if you are able to ride faster at a similar heart rate and/or power. Note that speed will be a function not only of your fitness but also of the weather conditions, so don't base your appraisal of your ride simply on speed, although that's one indicator. This is a very difficult workout, physically and mentally. You should only attempt this workout a few times during the season. Total workout length: 1.5 hours.

Modification: You can do an actual 40K time trial competition for this workout. See Workout 94.

Workout 18: Alternating 15-Second Intervals

Purpose of Workout: While short intervals are usually associated with anaerobic intervals, these are actually aerobic intervals. That's because the rest interval is equally short and you do not fully recover between intervals. Therefore, after a few of these, your heart rate should settle out at a threshold (zone 4) level. When you do this workout, record your heart rate if you can, and you will see that it levels out and may increase slightly throughout the session.

Course Description: This workout is best done on level or slightly rolling terrain. It's more difficult to maintain your targeted effort on hills. Choose either an out-and-back course or a loop that can be ridden multiple times to get in the allotted time. Try to avoid roads with lots of intersections, stop signs, stoplights, and traffic as these will interfere with your ability to ride without interruption.

Workout Description: Following a 10-minute warm-up in zone 2, increase the pace to zone 4 and hold this pace for 15 seconds. Then spin easily for 15 seconds. Repeat this pattern for 15 minutes. Take a 10-minute recovery spin in a low (easy) gear, then repeat another 15-minute set. Cool down for 10 minutes at the end. If you are basing your workout on heart rate, these intervals are too short for your heart rate to adapt, so you won't be able to judge your effort based on your heart rate. These intervals are only 15 seconds, and it takes your heart at least 20 seconds to catch up to your effort. You'll have to judge your effort more by feel, although your heart rate should stabilize in the zone 4 range after a few minutes. Total workout length: 1 hour.

Modification: You can also do these on an indoor trainer for a more controlled environment. You can do more or fewer intervals depending on your fitness level.

Workout 19: Alternating 30-Second Intervals

Purpose of Workout: While short intervals are usually associated with anaerobic intervals, these are actually aerobic intervals. That's because the rest interval is equally short and you do not fully recover between intervals. Therefore, after a few of these, your heart rate will settle out at a threshold (zone 4) level. When you do this, record your heart rate if you can, and you will see that it levels out and slightly increases throughout the session.

Course Description: This workout is best done on level or slightly rolling terrain. It's more difficult to maintain your targeted effort on hills. Choose either an out-and-back course or a loop that can be ridden multiple times to get in the interval session. Try to avoid roads with lots of intersections, stop signs, stoplights, and traffic as these will interfere with your ability to ride without too much interruption.

Workout Description: Following a 10-minute warm-up in zone 2, increase the pace to zone 4 and hold this pace for 30 seconds. Then spin easily for 30 seconds. Repeat this pattern for 15 minutes. Take a 10-minute recovery spin in a low (easy) gear and repeat the 15-minute set again. Cool down for 10 minutes at the end. If you are basing your workout on heart rate, these intervals are fairly short, so your heart rate won't get into zone 4 until the end of the 30-second interval. Therefore, you won't be able to judge your effort based on your heart rate, at least for the first 20 seconds of each interval. So, you'll have to judge your effort more by feel, but your heart rate should stabilize in the zone 4 range. Total workout length: 1 hour.

Modification: You can also do these on an indoor trainer for a more controlled environment. You can do more or fewer intervals depending on your fitness level.

Workout 20: Alternating 1-Minute Intervals

Purpose of Workout: These 1-minute intervals are aerobic intervals and are very helpful if you plan to ride time trials or compete in triathlons, or if you just want to be able to cruise along at a faster pace. By alternating 1 minute of effort in zone 4 with a recovery minute, you will be able to ride at your threshold pace longer than if you rode at a steady-state pace in zone 4. These intervals can be done to build up to a time trial pace. If you do time trials, this should be one of the basic workouts you do often.

Course Description: This workout is best done on level or slightly rolling terrain. It's more difficult to maintain your targeted effort on hills. Choose either an out-and-back course or a loop that can be ridden multiple times to get in the interval session. Try to avoid roads with lots of intersections, stop signs, stoplights, and traffic as these will interfere with your ability to ride without too much interruption.

Workout Description: Following a 10-minute warm-up in zone 2, increase the pace to zone 4 and hold this pace for 1 minute. Then spin easily for 1 minute. Repeat this pattern for 16 minutes, doing 8 intervals. Take a 10-minute spin and repeat the 16-minute set. Cool down for 10 minutes at the end. Target zone 4 for the duration of the 1-minute interval. Total workout length: 1.5 hours.

Modification: You can also do these on an indoor trainer for a more controlled environment. You can do more or fewer intervals depending on your fitness level.

Workout 21: Alternating 2-Minute Intervals

Purpose of Workout: These 2-minute intervals are actually aerobic intervals and are very helpful if you plan to ride time trials or compete in triathlons, or if you just want to be able to cruise along at a faster pace. By alternating 2 minutes of effort in zone 4 with 2 minutes of recovery, you will be able to ride at your threshold pace longer. If you do time trials, this should be one of the basic workouts that you do often; it can help you build up to a time trial effort.

Course Description: This workout is best done on level or slightly rolling terrain. It's more difficult to maintain your targeted effort on hills. Choose either an out-and-back course or a loop that can be ridden multiple times to get in the interval session. Try to avoid roads with lots of intersections, stop signs, stoplights, and traffic as these will interfere with your ability to ride without too much interruption.

Workout Description: Following a 10-minute warm-up in zone 2, increase the pace to zone 4 and hold this pace for 2 minutes. Then spin easily for 2 minutes. Repeat this pattern for 20 minutes. Take a 10-minute spin and repeat the 20-minute set. Cool down for 10 minutes at the end. Target zone 4 for the duration of the 2-minute interval. Total workout length: 1.5 hours.

Modification: You can also do these on an indoor trainer for a more controlled environment. You can do more or fewer intervals depending on your fitness level.

Workout 22: Alternating 3-Minute Intervals

Purpose of Workout: These 3-minute intervals are aerobic intervals and are very helpful if you plan to ride time trials or compete in triathlons, or if you just want to be able to cruise along at a faster pace. By alternating 3 minutes of effort in zone 4 with an equal 3 minutes of recovery, you will be able to ride at your threshold pace. In addition to helping you learn to ride at the threshold pace for 3 minutes, these will help you with your pacing. If you do time trials, this should be one of the basic workouts that you do often.

Course Description: This workout is best done on level or slightly rolling terrain. It's more difficult to maintain your targeted effort on hills. Choose either an out-and-back course or a loop that can be ridden multiple times to get in the interval session. Try to avoid roads with lots of intersections, stop signs, stoplights, and traffic as these will interfere with your ability to ride without too much interruption.

Workout Description: Following a 10-minute warm-up in zone 2, increase the pace to zone 4 and hold this pace for 3 minutes. Then spin easily for 3 minutes. Repeat this pattern for 18 minutes. Take a 10-minute recovery spin and repeat the 18-minute set. Cool down for 10 minutes at the end. Target zone 4 for the duration of the 3-minute interval. Total workout length: 1.5 hours.

Modification: You can also do these on an indoor trainer for a more controlled environment. You can do more or fewer intervals depending on your fitness level.

Workout 23: Decreasing Aerobic Intervals

Purpose of Workout: This series of aerobic intervals is meant to expose you to a wide range of durations of threshold efforts within a single workout. You start out by doing the longest effort and then decrease the length as you get more tired. These will help you to continue to push the zone 4 pace as you get fatigued. It also adds variety to the workout by doing different-length intervals in the same session.

Course Description: This workout is best done on level or slightly rolling terrain. It's more difficult to maintain your targeted effort on hills. Choose either an out-and-back course or a loop that can be ridden multiple times to get in the interval session. Try to avoid roads with lots of intersections, stop signs, stoplights, and traffic as these will interfere with your ability to ride without too much interruption.

Workout Description: Following a 10-minute warm-up in zone 2, increase the pace to zone 4 and hold this pace for 15 minutes. Spin easily for recovery for 10 minutes. Then do a 10-minute interval in zone 4 followed by a 5-minute recovery spin. Then do a 5-minute interval in zone 4 followed by a 2.5-minute recovery spin. Then do a 3-minute interval in zone 4 followed by a 2-minute recovery spin. Finally, do a 1-minute interval in zone 4. You should be able to maintain the same pace for these intervals all the way through the workout. Cool down for 10 minutes. Total workout length: 1.5 hours.

Modification: You can also do these on an indoor trainer for a more controlled environment. If you are very fit, you may repeat the whole sequence a second time.

Workout 24: Endurance Ride with 5-Minute Intervals

Purpose of Workout: This is very similar to Workout 6 within the Endurance Workouts chapter but is placed here to emphasize the high quality of the 5-minute aerobic intervals that are embedded within the endurance ride. The object of this workout is to provide aerobic threshold efforts during an endurance ride. This will help train you to be able to maintain a threshold pace during longer rides and as you get fatigued. These intervals also help break up the monotony of a long endurance ride.

Course Description: This workout is best done on level or rolling terrain. It's more difficult to maintain your threshold effort on hills. Choose either an out-and-back course or a loop that can be ridden multiple times to get in the interval session. Find a course that will allow you to ride your targeted distance.

Workout Description: During a zone 2 endurance ride, after a warm-up, ride at zone 2 for another 10 minutes then increase your effort to zone 4. Hold this pace for 5 minutes then resume zone 2 pace for 10 more minutes. Then do another 5-minute zone 4 effort. Repeat this sequence of 10 minutes in zone 2 followed by 5 minutes in zone 4 for the duration of the ride. Cool down in zone 1–2 for 10 minutes at the end of the ride. Total workout length: 1–3 hours.

Modification: This is a good workout to do on an endurance ride on your trainer in the winter. It breaks up the long ride and gives you something to think about.

Workout 25: Endurance Ride with 10-Minute Intervals

Purpose of Workout: This could also be put within the Endurance Workouts chapter, but it is here because the emphasis really is on the 10-minute aerobic intervals that are embedded within the endurance ride. The object of this workout is to provide aerobic threshold efforts during an endurance ride. This will help train you to be able to maintain a threshold pace during longer rides and as you get fatigued. These intervals also help break up the monotony of a long endurance ride.

Course Description: This workout is best done on level or rolling terrain. It's more difficult to maintain your threshold effort on hills. Choose either an out-and-back course or a loop that can be ridden multiple times to get in the interval session. Find a course that will allow you to ride your targeted distance.

Workout Description: During a zone 2 endurance ride, after a warm-up, ride in zone 2 for 20 minutes then increase your effort to zone 4. Hold this pace for 10 minutes then resume zone 2 pace for 20 more minutes. Then do another 10-minute zone 4 effort. Repeat this sequence of 20 minutes in zone 2 followed by 10 minutes in zone 4 for the duration of the ride. Cool down in zone 1–2 for 10 minutes at the end. Total workout length: 1–3 hours.

Modification: This is a good workout to do on an endurance ride on your trainer in the winter. It breaks up the long ride and gives you something to think about.

Workout 26: 6-Minute Uphill Intervals

Purpose of Workout: This workout uses a mild uphill to help provide resistance to complete a 6-minute threshold interval. It is similar to Workout 12 but uses a hill instead of being done on a level road. This will help train you both physically and mentally to sustain your threshold pace while going up a grade, which is common in time trials and triathlons.

Course Description: Find a gradual (3–5% grade) incline of about 2 miles in length. If you don't have such a hill, see Workout 27 for an alternative.

Workout Description: Warm up thoroughly and then begin riding up the hill at zone 4 pace. Keep your cadence up to 85–95 RPM throughout the interval. It should take you 5 to 6 minutes to ride up this hill. Turn around and spin easily going back down the hill. If you pace it right, you take just as long going down as up. Repeat this hill interval 3 more times. Spin to cool down for 10 minutes. Total workout length: 1.25 hours.

Modification: This can also be done on an indoor trainer. Increase the resistance or use a larger gear for 5 to 6 minutes at a time, then spin an equal amount of time between intervals.

Workout 27: 6-Minute Headwind Intervals

Purpose of Workout: This workout uses the wind to help provide resistance to complete a 6-minute threshold interval. It is similar to Workout 26 but uses the wind instead of a hill, in case you don't have a 2-mile grade available. It also gives you an option to use on a very windy day, when you might ordinarily decide against riding. This will help train you both physically and mentally to sustain your threshold pace while going into a headwind, which is always a good skill to have, especially during a time trial.

Course Description: Use a level or gently rolling stretch of road about 2 miles in length. If you choose a hilly course, the hill combined with the headwind will make it very difficult to maintain your cadence and pace. Select a day with a wind of at least 15 miles per hour and find a road that allows you to ride into the headwind in one direction for 2 miles. You will turn around and recover riding back with a tailwind.

Workout Description: Warm up thoroughly and then begin riding into the headwind at zone 4 pace. Keep your cadence up to 85–95 RPM throughout the interval. Ride for 6 minutes or 2 miles at this pace. Turn around and spin easily, going back with the tailwind. Repeat this headwind interval 3 more times. Spin to cool down for 10 minutes. Total workout length: 1.25 hours.

Workout 28: 2-Person Time Trials

Purpose of Workout: A great way to get in a good threshold workout is to ride a 2-person time trial. You need to find someone of similar ability. By riding together and sharing the draft, you will be able to keep up a hard but sustainable pace. Having each other will continue to ensure that you push each other and keep the pace high. This should allow you to maintain a threshold pace.

Course Description: Almost any course will work, although very hilly courses will make it difficult to maintain a constant pace. It should be as free of intersections as possible to allow you to maintain a steady pace with minimal interruptions so you can concentrate on drafting.

Workout Description: Warm up thoroughly and then begin riding your time trial. Take turns at the front. When in the front, you will do more work as you are in the wind. When you rotate to the back position, you can take advantage of the draft and recover a little. Pulls at the front should be between 20 and 30 seconds. Avoid taking pulls longer than this as your speed will tend to drop. Your heart rate may go up and down a little as you move from front to back, but it should be within zone 4 for most of the ride. Total workout length: 1 to 2 hours.

Modification: If you don't have a training partner with whom to do this workout, you can mimic this workout by yourself. Alternate slightly harder efforts with slightly easier efforts, both in zone 4 range, throughout your ride. This is in fact similar to Workout 19.

Chapter 6
Anaerobic Workouts

Anaerobic workouts are really for fine-tuning your fitness. You need to have developed a good aerobic base before attempting these workouts by doing endurance, tempo, and aerobic threshold workouts for several weeks. For some cyclists, such as recreational riders who just want to ride at endurance pace for tours, anaerobic workouts may not even be necessary. But even if not necessary for your type of riding, you might consider these just to add some challenge and variety to your training. These are the workouts that will give you peak fitness and push you to new levels. They allow you to keep up with accelerations, climb hills fast, and be competitive in races. Keep in mind that these are very intense workouts and will get your heart rate up close to its maximum. ***Therefore, it's very important that you have a solid aerobic base and have clearance from your physician before attempting these workouts.*** During your main cycling season, you can do these 1 or 2 times a week. Because they are so intense, do not do these more than 2 days per week and allow ample rest days to recover. Depending on your fitness, you may choose to do 1 of these workouts per week during the off-season as well, but only after you have done at least 1 year of training first. These workouts increase the ability to get oxygen to your muscles (VO2 max) and the ability to ride past your aerobic threshold.

Workout 29: Alternating 2-Minute Intervals

Purpose of Workout: This workout is similar to Workout 21 (aerobic 2-minute intervals), but the difference is that these 2-minute intervals need to be done with more effort to move you into zone 5. The 2 minutes of recovery should be an easy to moderate effort and allow you to recover enough to repeat a hard effort multiple times. You will, however, become more fatigued, and lactic acid will build up over the course of these intervals, which is the intent. This workout will train you to push into your anaerobic zone, build recovery, and improve your lactate tolerance. This workout should only be attempted after a good aerobic base has been established.

Course Description: Almost any course will work, although very hilly courses will make it difficult to maintain your desired effort during the intervals. This can be a continuous route or a short loop on which you do many laps. Low-traffic loops in parks are very conducive to this type of interval workout.

Workout Description: Warm up thoroughly for 15 minutes. Begin your 2-minute intervals and strive to reach zone 5 heart rate by the end of the first minute and hold that effort for the second minute. Then pedal easily for 2 minutes; try to get your heart rate down to zone 2–3 during each rest interval. Repeat the zone 5 intervals as long as you can until you can't achieve zone 5 effort any longer. As you become fitter, you will be able to do more of these. Total workout length: 1–1.5 hours.

Modification: This is a good workout for those times when you need to ride inside on your trainer. The controlled environment allows you to do very specific intervals.

Workout 30: 1-Minute Intervals

Purpose of Workout: Unlike Workout 20 (aerobic 1-minute intervals), these intervals are meant to be very intense 1-minute efforts that get you to zone 5, followed by a 1-minute recovery interval so as to allow you to do another hard interval after the recovery. This workout is intended to train you to ride faster and harder, tolerate lactic acid, and push through fatigue as these intervals continue. These are very helpful if you intend to race criteriums or road races. This workout should only be attempted after a good aerobic base has been established.

Course Description: Almost any course will work, although very hilly courses will make it difficult to maintain your desired effort during the intervals. This can be a continuous route or a short loop on which you do many laps. Often, low-traffic loops, such as in parks, are very conducive to this type of interval workout.

Workout Description: Warm up thoroughly for 15 minutes. Begin your 1-minute intervals and strive to reach zone 5 heart rate by the end of the minute. Then pedal easily for 1 minute; try to get your heart rate down to zone 2–3 during each rest interval. Repeat the zone 5 intervals as long as you can until you can't achieve zone 5 effort any longer. As you get fitter, you will be able to do more of these. Total workout length: 1–1.5 hours.

Modification: This is a good workout for those times when you need to ride inside on your trainer. The controlled environment allows you to do very specific intervals.

Workout 31: 30-Second Intervals

Purpose of Workout: Unlike Workout 19 (aerobic 30-second intervals), these intervals are meant to be very intense 30-second efforts and are followed by 30 seconds of easy spinning to allow some, but not complete, recovery. This workout is intended to train you to ride faster and harder repeatedly, tolerate lactic acid, and push through fatigue as these intervals continue. These are very helpful if you intend to race criteriums or road races. This workout should only be attempted after a good aerobic base has been established.

Course Description: Almost any course will work, although very hilly courses will make it difficult to maintain your desired effort. This can be a continuous route or a short loop on which you do many laps. Often, low-traffic loops, such as in parks, are very conducive to this type of interval workout.

Workout Description: Warm up thoroughly for 15 minutes. Begin your 30-second intervals at zone 5 pace. Because of the short duration of these intervals, your heart rate will not reach zone 5 level in 30 seconds. Unless you have a power meter, you will have to judge your effort more by feel, but it should feel close to an all-out effort. During each recovery phase, pedal easily for 30 seconds to allow your heart rate to get down to zone 3. Repeat the zone 5 intervals as long as you can until you can't put out a hard effort any longer. Your heart rate and fatigue will increase throughout this set of intervals. As you become fitter, you will be able to do more of these intervals. Total workout length: 1–1.5 hours.

Modification: This is a good workout for those times when you need to ride inside on your trainer. The controlled environment allows you to do very specific intervals.

Workout 32: 15-Second Intervals

Purpose of Workout: Unlike Workout 18 (aerobic 15-second intervals), these intervals are meant to be very intense 15-second anaerobic efforts and are followed by 15 seconds of easy spinning to allow some, but not complete, recovery. This workout is intended to train you to ride faster and harder repeatedly, build lactic acid tolerance, and push through fatigue as these intervals continue. These are very helpful if you intend to race criteriums or road races. This workout should only be attempted after a good aerobic base has been established.

Course Description: Almost any course will work, although very hilly courses will make it difficult to maintain your desired effort. This can be a continuous route or a short loop on which you do many laps. Often, low-traffic loops, such as in parks, are very conducive to this type of interval workout.

Workout Description: Warm up thoroughly for 15 minutes. Begin your 15-second intervals at zone 5 pace. Because of the short duration of these intervals, your heart rate will not reach zone 5 level in 15 seconds. Unless you have a power meter, you will have to judge your effort more by feel, but it should be close to an all-out effort. During the 15-second recovery phase, pedal easily and try to get your heart rate down to zone 3–4 during this rest interval. Repeat the zone 5 intervals as long as you can until you can't put out a hard effort any longer. Recover for 10 minutes of easy spinning and do another set of these intervals. As you become fitter, you will be able to do more of these. Total workout length: 1–1.5 hours.

Modification: This is a good workout for those times when you need to ride inside on your trainer. The controlled environment allows you to do very specific intervals.

Workout 33: Endurance Ride
with 1-Minute Intervals

Purpose of Workout: This could equally be put under the Endurance Workouts section, but it is here because the emphasis is on the 1-minute anaerobic intervals that are embedded within this endurance ride. The object of this workout is to provide short anaerobic efforts during a long ride. This will help train you to be able to put out very hard efforts during longer rides and as you get fatigued, such as during a road race. These intervals also help break up the monotony of a long endurance ride.

Course Description: This workout can be done on almost any terrain. Pick a course that allows you to ride the distance desired. If it happens to be hilly, that's okay. You can use the hills for your 1-minute intervals if you wish. If hills don't come along exactly every 15 minutes, you can do a hard 1-minute interval a little more randomly as the hills do come along.

Workout Description: During a zone 2 endurance ride, after a warm-up, ride in zone 2 for 15 minutes then stand and increase speed and effort rapidly to zone 5. Sit and hold this pace for 1 minute then resume zone 2 pace for 14 more minutes. Then do another 1-minute zone 5 effort. Repeat this sequence of 14 minutes in zone 2 followed by 1 minute in zone 5 for the duration of the ride. Cool down in zone 1–2 for 10 minutes at the end. Total workout length: 1–3 hours.

Modification: This can be done with others on a group ride as long as you explain what you are doing. Hopefully they will join in with you and help make these efforts even harder. It's always easier to push hard when riding with others.

Workout 34: Endurance Ride
with 3-Minute Intervals

Purpose of Workout: This could equally be put under the Endurance Workouts section, but it is here because the emphasis is on the 3-minute anaerobic intervals embedded within this endurance ride. The object of this workout is to provide anaerobic efforts during a long ride. This will help train you to be able to put out very hard efforts during longer rides and as you get fatigued. These intervals also help break up the monotony of a long endurance ride.

Course Description: This workout can be done on almost any terrain. Pick a course that allows you to ride the distance desired. If it happens to be hilly, that's okay. You can use the hills for your 3-minute intervals. If the hills don't come along every 17 minutes, you can do a hard 3-minute interval a little more randomly as the hills do come along.

Workout Description: During a zone 2 endurance ride, after a warm-up, ride in zone 2 for 17 minutes then increase speed and effort rapidly to zone 5. Hold this pace for 3 minutes then resume zone 2 pace for 17 more minutes. Then do another 3-minute zone 5 effort. Repeat this sequence of 17 minutes in zone 2 followed by 3 minutes in zone 5 for the duration of the ride. Cool down in zone 1–2 for 10 minutes at the end. Total workout length: 1–3 hours.

Modification: This can be done with others on a group ride as long as you explain what you are doing. Hopefully they will join in with you and make these efforts even harder. It's always easier to push hard when riding with others.

Workout 35: 30-Second VO2 Max Intervals

Purpose of Workout: This workout is designed to increase your top-end speed and maximum ability to ride fast. This pushes your body's ability to generate work by increasing its ability to pump blood and consume oxygen. These are very hard efforts and should only be attempted after a good aerobic base has been established.

Course Description: This workout is best done on a fairly flat road with few stops and little traffic so as to be able to concentrate on high-quality intervals. A loop within a park or quiet neighborhood works well.

Workout Description: Warm up very thoroughly, at least 15 minutes. Each interval should be started off very explosively and ridden as hard as possible for the 30 seconds. You may stand for the first 5 to 10 seconds and then sit for the remainder. Once the interval is over, shift to an easier gear and spin for 2 minutes. The objective during this recovery period is to get your breathing and heart rate back to as low a rate as possible and to be ready for a hard effort in the next interval. Spinning a low gear will help flush the muscles out and encourage blood flow. Repeat 9 more times. If you are very fit, take a 10-minute recovery spin and repeat another set of 10 intervals. Warm down. Total workout length: 1–1.5 hours.

Modification: This can be done with others as long as they are of similar ability. It's always easier to push hard when riding with others. But don't ease up on the efforts if you are stronger than your training partner(s).

Workout 36: 1-Minute VO2 Max Intervals

Purpose of Workout: This workout is designed to increase your top-end speed and maximum ability to ride fast. This pushes your body's ability to generate work by increasing its ability to pump blood and consume oxygen. These are very hard efforts and should only be attempted after a good aerobic base has been established.

Course Description: This workout is best done on a fairly flat road with few stops and little traffic so as to be able to concentrate on high-quality intervals. A loop within a park or quiet neighborhood works well.

Workout Description: Warm up very thoroughly, at least 15 minutes. Each interval should be started off very explosively and ridden as hard as possible for the 1 minute. You may want to stand for the first 5 to 10 seconds and then sit for the remainder. Once the interval is over, shift to an easier gear and spin for 2 minutes. The objective during this recovery period is to get your breathing and heart rate back as low as possible and to minimize the buildup of lactic acid so as to be ready for the next interval. Spinning a low gear will help flush the muscles out and encourage blood flow. Repeat 6 more times. If you are very fit, take a 10-minute recovery spin and repeat another set of 7 intervals. Warm down. Total workout length: 1–1.5 hours.

Modification: This can be done with others as long as they are of similar ability. It's always easier to push hard when riding with others. But don't ease up on the efforts if you are stronger than your training partner(s).

Workout 37: 2-Minute VO2 Max Intervals

Purpose of Workout: This workout is similar to Workout 29, but the main difference is the harder effort during each interval and a longer recovery period in this workout. To be able to put out a maximal effort during the relatively long 2-minute intervals, you need to be fairly well recovered, so the recovery period is 4 minutes during these intervals. This workout is designed to increase your top-end speed and your ability to hold that speed for 2 minutes. This pushes your body's ability to generate work by increasing its ability to pump blood and consume oxygen. These are very hard efforts and should only be attempted after a good aerobic base has been established.

Course Description: This workout is best done on a fairly flat road with few stops and little traffic so as to be able to concentrate on high-quality intervals. A loop within a park or quiet neighborhood works well.

Workout Description: Warm up very thoroughly, at least 15 minutes. Each interval should be started off very explosively and be ridden as hard as possible for the entire 2 minutes. Once the interval is over, shift to an easier gear and spin for 4 minutes. The objective during this recovery period is to get your breathing and heart rate back as low as possible and to minimize the buildup of lactic acid so as to be ready for the next interval. Spinning a low gear will help flush the muscles out and encourage blood flow. Repeat 4 more times. If you are very fit, take a 10-minute recovery spin and repeat another set of 5 intervals. Warm down. Total workout length: 1–1.5 hours.

Modification: This can be done with others as long as they are of similar ability. It's always easier to push hard when riding with others. But don't ease up on the efforts if you are stronger than your training partner(s).

Workout 38: Increasing Pyramid Intervals

Purpose of Workout: This workout trains you to ride a hard pace at varying durations with varying recovery times. It's an all-around good anaerobic workout. This pushes your body's ability to generate work by increasing its ability to pump blood, consume oxygen, and tolerate lactic acid buildup. These are very hard efforts and should only be attempted after a good aerobic base has been established.

Course Description: This workout is best done on a fairly flat road with few stops and little traffic so as to be able to concentrate on high-quality intervals. A loop within a park or quiet neighborhood works well.

Workout Description: Warm up very thoroughly, at least 15 minutes. Start with a hard zone 5 effort for 30 seconds and then spin easily for 30 seconds. Then do a 1-minute interval followed by 1 minute of easy spinning. Repeat this sequence, each time increasing the duration by 30 seconds for both the zone 5 interval and recovery period: 0:30, 1:00, 1:30, 2:00, 2:30, 3:00; and then come back down: 2:30, 2:00, 1:30, 1:00, 0:30. If you are very fit, a second set can be attempted. Warm down. Total workout length: 1–1.5 hours.

Modification: This is a great workout to do on an indoor trainer because it requires a lot of concentration on your watch, and it's easier to do that inside where there aren't distractions and traffic with which to contend.

Workout 39: Decreasing Pyramid Intervals

Purpose of Workout: This workout trains you to ride a hard pace for varying durations with varying recovery times. It's an all-around good anaerobic workout. It is very similar to Workout 38, but it is done in reverse—the longer intervals are done twice and the shorter ones only once, resulting in an even harder workout. This pushes your body's ability to generate work by increasing its ability to pump blood, consume oxygen, and tolerate lactic acid buildup. These are very hard efforts and should only be attempted after a good aerobic base has been established.

Course Description: This workout is best done on a fairly flat road with few stops and little traffic so as to be able to concentrate on high-quality intervals. A loop within a park or quiet neighborhood works well.

Workout Description: Warm up very thoroughly, at least 15 minutes. Start with a hard zone 5 effort for 3 minutes and then spin easily for 3 minutes. Then do a 2:30 interval followed by 2:30 of spinning. Repeat this sequence, each time decreasing the duration by 30 seconds for both the zone 5 interval and recovery period: 3:00, 2:30, 2:00, 1:30, 1:00, 0:30; and then come back up: 1:00, 1:30, 2:00, 2:30, 3:00. If you are very fit, a second set can be attempted. Warm down. Total workout length: 1–1.5 hours.

Modification: This is a great workout to do on an indoor trainer because it requires a lot of concentration on your watch, and it's easier to do that inside where there aren't distractions and traffic to contend with.

Workout 40: Increasing Intervals

Purpose of Workout: This workout trains you to ride a hard pace for varying durations with varying recovery times. It's an all-around good anaerobic workout. It is very similar to Workout 38 but is done in one direction—the longer intervals are done toward the end as you get more tired, resulting in a hard effort required to complete these. This pushes your body's ability to generate work by increasing its ability to pump blood, consume oxygen, and tolerate lactic acid. These are very hard efforts and should only be attempted after a good aerobic base has been established.

Course Description: This workout is best done on a fairly flat road with few stops and little traffic so as to be able to concentrate on high-quality intervals. A loop within a park or quiet neighborhood works well.

Workout Description: Warm up very thoroughly, at least 15 minutes. Start with a hard zone 5 effort for 30 seconds, and then spin easily for 30 seconds. Then do a 1-minute interval followed by 1 minute of spinning. Repeat this sequence, each time increasing the duration by 30 seconds for both the zone 5 interval and recovery period: 0:30, 1:00, 1:30, 2:00, 2:30, all the way up to 5:00. If you are very fit, a second set can be attempted. Warm down. Total workout length: 1–1.5 hours.

Modification: This is a great workout to do on an indoor trainer because it requires a lot of concentration on your watch, and it's easier to do that inside where there aren't distractions and traffic to contend with.

Workout 41: Decreasing Intervals

Purpose of Workout: This workout trains you to ride a hard pace for varying durations with varying recovery times. It's an all-around good anaerobic workout. It is very similar to Workout 40 but is done in the opposite direction—the shorter intervals are done toward the end as you get more tired, hopefully allowing you to maintain the same or increasing effort throughout the workout. This pushes your body's ability to generate work by increasing its ability to pump blood, consume oxygen, and tolerate lactic acid buildup. These are very hard efforts and should only be attempted after a good aerobic base has been established.

Course Description: This workout is best done on a fairly flat road with few stops and little traffic so as to be able to concentrate on high-quality intervals. A loop within a park or quiet neighborhood works well.

Workout Description: Warm up very thoroughly, at least 15 minutes. Start with a hard zone 5 effort for 5 minutes and then spin easily for 5 minutes. Then do a 4:30 interval followed by 4:30 of spinning. Repeat this sequence, each time decreasing the duration by 30 seconds for both the zone 5 interval and recovery period: 5:00, 4:30, 4:00, 3:30, 2:00, all the way down to 0:30. If you are extremely fit, a second set can be attempted. Warm down. Total workout length: 1–1.5 hours.

Modification: This is a great workout to do on an indoor trainer because it requires a lot of concentration on your watch, and it's easier to do that inside where there aren't distractions and traffic to contend with.

Workout 42: Random Intervals and Recovery Periods

Purpose of Workout: This workout trains you to ride a hard pace for varying durations with varying recovery times. It's an all-around good anaerobic workout. The length of the intervals and recovery periods are randomized, creating a variable workout with varying levels of fatigue being built up. At some points, you may have more time spent in zone 5 effort than you do in recovery; at other times the opposite may occur. This simulates the situation you will face in races, especially criteriums.

Course Description: This workout can really only effectively be done on an indoor trainer. You have to have full concentration on your watch and your order of intervals and recovery. You will need to figure out how to attach your sheet of paper with the order of intervals near your bike so you can refer to it during the workout.

Workout Description: Prior to the workout, you will need to determine the order of intervals and recovery periods. The method I use is to take a die (one of a pair of dice) and roll it. If it comes up a "1," that means 30 seconds, "2" = 1 minute, "3" = 1.5 minutes, etc., up to "6," which equals 3 minutes. So the intervals and recovery periods will range from 0:30 to 3:00. Your first throw is the first interval; the second throw is the first recovery period, and so on. Write these down and continue this process until you have 45 minutes' worth of intervals and recovery. Warm up for 15 minutes then begin your workout following the pre-written set of intervals and recovery periods. Warm down. Total workout length: 1 hour.

Modification: You can also do this with a group in an indoor group training session. Have the leader call out each interval and rest period throughout the workout. This adds an element of surprise for the group as they do not know what is coming next.

Workout 43: Criterium Intervals

Purpose of Workout: This workout trains you to ride a hard pace at short, frequent intervals using an actual short loop course to simulate a criterium race. These intervals should be very intense, with equally short recovery periods. The purpose is to build up and learn to ride through lactic acid accumulation. This is a very intense workout (primarily for competitors) and should only be attempted after a good base fitness has been developed.

Course Description: Find a short course with several corners, one corner every block or so. This workout is best done in a quiet neighborhood or in a business section of town after business hours, where there won't be much traffic. The course can be flat or have some moderate grades in it. It's also better to do these doing right turns so as to avoid riding through intersections across traffic.

Workout Description: Warm up very thoroughly, at least 15 minutes. Begin riding the course. As you ride out of each corner, stay seated and accelerate up to close to your top-end speed and hold that pace for another 10 seconds. Total duration of the interval should be about 20 seconds. Ease up and ride through the next corner, then accelerate again. Repeat these short but intense efforts as you come out of every corner for a total of 15 minutes. Take 10 minutes to ride easily, then repeat the 15 minutes of hard efforts again. Warm down. Total workout length: 1 hour.

Modification: If you would prefer, or as you get tired, it's okay to stand briefly to accelerate out of the corners.

Workout 44: Fartlek Speedplay

Purpose of Workout: *Fartlek* means "speed play" in Swedish and is a form of training where the intensity varies randomly. It is most often used in reference to running, but it also works with cycling. This workout is unstructured and you let the course and terrain determine your pace and effort. The result is a mixture of aerobic (threshold) and anaerobic paces. This workout puts stress on both your aerobic and anaerobic systems with variable recovery rates. It trains you to ride at a high but variable pace. It's also a fun workout because it is less structured and lets you ride in varied terrain and take advantage of it.

Course Description: This workout can be done on almost any course. It actually works better when done in town where there are a lot of stop signs, corners, traffic, and hills of various length and steepness with which to work.

Workout Description: Warm up very thoroughly, at least 15 minutes. As you conduct this workout, use the course to determine your efforts. When leaving from a stop sign or red light, stand and accelerate and hold that pace for 15 seconds then sit back down and pedal at a moderate pace. When you come to hills, accelerate up and over them. On longer flat sections, you may choose to sprint to a traffic sign along the route or do zone 5 intervals between chosen telephone poles. Try to get to a zone 5 pace or even occasionally zone 6 during this ride. Total workout length: 1–1.5 hours.

Modification: If you are fortunate enough not to have stop signs, traffic, hills, etc., you can still do this workout just by using your cycling computer. Decide to sprint or do an interval whenever your speed drops below a selected speed, such as 18 MPH. When you slow down due to a hill, headwind, or traffic signs, you increase your effort until you can get your speed above your selected target.

Workout 45: Standing Short Hill Intervals

Purpose of Workout: This workout is both a strength and anaerobic workout. It's in this section because its real intent is to provide a serious anaerobic workout to train you to ride hard and fast up shorter, steeper hills. You will keep your cadence high on this ride (85 RPM or higher) to avoid a lot of leg strain and to focus on keeping the heart rate high. Specific leg strength hill workouts can be found in Chapter 8.

Course Description: You will need to find a short but fairly steep hill for this workout. The hill should be about a quarter mile in length and have a 5–8% grade. This is steep enough to force you out of your saddle and to work hard. You can use a circuit if you have one with 1 or more hills on it, or you can use 1 hill and go up and down the same one, which is boring but effective.

Workout Description: Warm up very thoroughly, at least 15 minutes. As you approach the hill, select a gear that will allow you to spin at least 85 RPM for most of the hill (you may slow down near the top). Stand and accelerate all the way up the hill, concentrating on maintaining a smooth continuous pedal stroke while standing. Avoid wobbling all over the bike. At the top, sit, downshift, and spin for 3 minutes. Then repeat the hill interval, working up to 10–12 intervals as your fitness improves. You should be reaching zone 5–6 during these intervals. Warm down. Total workout length: 1 hour.

Workout 46: Seated Short Hill Intervals

Purpose of Workout: Because it's done on hills, this workout is both a strength and an anaerobic workout. It's in this section because it's a really good workout to get your heart rate into zone 5. It will train you to ride hard and fast up shorter, steeper hills while seated. You will keep your cadence high on this ride (85 RPM or higher) to avoid a lot of leg strain and to keep the heart rate high. Specific leg strength hill workouts can be found in Chapter 8.

Course Description: You will need to find a short but fairly steep hill for this workout. The hill should be about a quarter mile in length and contain a 5–8% grade. This is steep enough to force you to work very hard. You can use a circuit if you have one with 1 or more hills on it, or you can use 1 hill and go up and down the same one.

Workout Description: Warm up very thoroughly, at least 15 minutes. As you approach the hill, select a gear that will allow you to spin at least 85 RPM for most of the hill (you may slow down near the top). Stay seated and accelerate all the way up the hill, concentrating on maintaining a smooth circular pedal stroke while standing. At the top, downshift and spin for 5 minutes. Then repeat the hill interval, working up to 10–12 intervals as your fitness improves. You should be reaching zone 5–6 during these intervals. Warm down. Total workout length: 1 hour.

Chapter 7
Sprint and Power Workouts

Sprint and power workouts are the icing on the cake, in terms of building fitness. After you have a solid aerobic and endurance base and have been doing anaerobic intervals, sprint and power workouts give you that razor-edge finish to your fitness. Unless you race, you probably won't need to do these workouts, and you may not have the solid base fitness on which to do these. But if you have developed good fitness and want to experiment, give these a try. Keep in mind that these are extremely intense workouts and will get your heart rate up to its maximum. ***Therefore, it's very important that you have a solid aerobic and anaerobic base and have clearance from your physician before attempting these workouts.*** If you are a competitive road cyclist, you will need to do 1 or 2 of these workouts each week during the competitive season. There really isn't a need to do these in the base or off-season as these get you to your peak level of fitness and it's impossible to maintain that level of fitness for the entire season.

Workout 47: Sprints

Purpose of Workout: This workout is simply to improve your sprinting ability—your top-end speed and duration. Typically, racers will do this sort of workout, but even if you don't compete, you might find it interesting and fun to do once in a while. It is designed to make you work at your maximum ability for short periods of time, while practicing the sprinting technique. You will want to be fully recovered between sprints to be able to produce a maximal effort during the sprints.

Course Description: It's best to find a course that is fairly level and has low traffic so you don't have to worry about vehicles. When you are going all out in a sprint, you don't want to have to contend with anything else in the road. Scout out your course and identify landmarks to which you will sprint, whether they are specific telephone poles, driveways, or road signs. These sprints should be several miles apart. Many cyclists have a tradition of sprinting to "Stop Ahead" road signs. If this describes you, you can easily incorporate Stop Ahead sprints into your ride, or use other traffic landmarks and road signs.

Workout Description: Warm up thoroughly for at least 15 minutes. Roll along and pick up speed as you approach your sprint. Put your hands on the lower bend of your handlebars. Build up to a high speed such as 25 MPH, shift to your sprinting gear, and then stand and explode as you sprint to your designated sprint point. Push down hard and also remember to pull up and forward with the other foot. After about 7 to 10 pedal strokes, sit down and continue to accelerate throughout the sprint. These sprints should last 20–30 seconds. Shift to an easier gear and spin for at least 5 minutes before starting your next sprint. Start out doing 4 or 5 sprints and work your way up to 8 or 10 as you get fitter. Cool down for 10 minutes. Total workout length: 1 hour.

Modification: You can also do these on a slight downhill or with a tailwind for more leg speed. You can also do these with others as they tend to push you to sprint harder than when alone.

Workout 48: Seated Accelerations

Purpose of Workout: This workout is intended to improve your ability to build leg strength to accelerate quickly and powerfully from a seated position. This will give you more strength and speed to accelerate while seated in a paceline or going up a short hill.

Course Description: Find a stretch of road that is flat. You will do these accelerations as intervals, so you can ride back and forth on the same stretch of road or around a flat loop.

Workout Description: Warm up thoroughly for at least 15 minutes. Shift to a large gear, one of your largest. Slow down to about 5 MPH and then rapidly accelerate while staying seated. At first your cadence will be very slow, but the idea is to increase your cadence up to 100 or more RPMs during each interval. Try to smoothly yet strongly increase your cadence and speed. Once you can no longer accelerate and increase your speed or cadence, the interval is done. These intervals should only last 15–25 seconds. Spin easily for 5 or more minutes before attempting the next interval. Start out doing 5 of these per session and work up to 10. Cool down for 10 minutes. Total workout length: 1 hour.

Modification: Try these on a slight to moderate slope or into a headwind for added resistance.

Workout 49: CP Jumps

Purpose of Workout: CP stands for creatine phosphate, an energy compound in your body that provides for the immediate expenditure of high amounts of energy during a sudden burst of effort. Once you exert for more than 10 seconds, your anaerobic system takes over as the primary energy source. Training your CP system is useful especially for races that require extremely intense, repeated bursts of effort such as for sprinting, attacking, or climbing short hills. This is a very intense workout (primarily for competitors) and should only be attempted after a good base fitness has been developed.

Course Description: This workout can be done on almost any terrain, but a road with little traffic is best. It can be done on short hills or flat roads. It's one of the few workouts that cannot be done on a trainer, due to the explosive force required.

Workout Description: Warm up thoroughly for at least 15 minutes. Roll along and pick up speed as you approach your interval. Similar to the Sprints Workout (Workout 47), build up to a high speed such as 25 MPH, shift to your sprinting gear, and then stand and explode as you accelerate as hard and fast as possible with maximal effort. Push down hard and also remember to pull up and forward with the other foot. These sprints should last 10–12 seconds only and should be done standing all the way. Once you can no longer accelerate while standing, you are finished with the interval. Shift to an easier gear and spin for at least 5 minutes before starting your next interval. Start out doing 4 or 5 intervals and work your way up to 6 to 8 as you become fitter. Cool down for 10 minutes. Total workout length: 1 hour.

Workout 50: Standing Hill Sprints

Purpose of Workout: This workout involves very short, intense efforts. While it is done on hills and does help build leg strength, its primary purpose is to develop your ability to put out an extremely large amount of energy for short amounts of time. This is similar to Workout 45, but these sprints are shorter and even more intense (zone 6). This is a very intense workout (primarily for competitors) and should only be attempted after a good base fitness has been developed.

Course Description: You will need to find a short but steep hill for this workout. The hill should be about a quarter mile in length and contain at least an 8% grade. This is steep enough to provide the resistance needed for an explosive effort. You can use a circuit if you have one with 1 or more hills on it, or you can use 1 hill and go up and down the same one.

Workout Description: Warm up very thoroughly, at least 15 minutes. As you approach the hill, select a gear that will allow you to spin at about 75 RPM. Stand and explosively accelerate all the way up the hill, concentrating on pushing and pulling on the pedals. At the top, sit, downshift, and spin for 5 minutes. Then repeat the hill sprint, working up to 10–12 intervals as your fitness improves. You should be reaching zone 5–6 by the end of these intervals. Warm down. Total workout length: 1 hour.

Workout 51: Seated Hill Intervals with Sprint at Top

Purpose of Workout: While similar to Workout 46, this differs because the focus is not so much on the seated hill climbing part but the standing explosive sprint across the top of the hill. Normally riders slow down toward the top of a hill. This workout will train you to attack up and over the top of a hill while others are easing up. This not only develops your strength and power, but also gives you mental confidence to do so in a race, or at least to have the stamina to follow an attack on a hill. This is a very intense workout (primarily for competitors) and should only be attempted after a good base fitness has been developed.

Course Description: You will need to find a short but fairly steep hill for this workout. The hill should be about a quarter mile in length and contain a 5–8% grade. Ideally, it should be less steep near the bottom and become steeper towards the top. You can use a circuit if you have one with 1 or more hills on it, or you can use 1 hill and go up and down the same one.

Workout Description: Warm up very thoroughly for at least 15 minutes. As you approach the hill, select a gear that will allow you to spin at least 85 RPM for most of the hill. Stay seated and accelerate up the hill, concentrating on maintaining a smooth circular pedal stroke). About ¾ of the way to the top, shift into a larger (harder) gear, stand, and attack up the rest of the hill. Don't stop riding as the hill crests but continue to push all the way until the hill levels out or begins to go back down. After each interval, downshift and spin for 5 minutes. Then repeat the interval, working up to 10 intervals as your fitness improves. You should be reaching zone 6 during these intervals. Warm down. Total workout length: 1.5 hours.

Modification: You can also throw in these hilltop sprints on longer hills that you may come across on your endurance rides, to add a power component to those rides.

Workout 52: Criterium Jumps

Purpose of Workout: While similar to Workout 43, this workout focuses more on the sprint or jump coming out of the corners. This workout trains you to accelerate with power over and over again, as in a criterium. Because the focus is on force and power, these are short and are only a few seconds long. These intervals should be very intense, with somewhat longer recovery periods. This is a very intense workout (primarily for competitors) and should only be attempted after a good base fitness has been developed.

Course Description: Find a short course with several corners, each corner a block or so apart. These are best done in a quiet neighborhood or a business section of town after business hours, where there won't be much traffic. The course can be flat or have some moderate grades in it. It's also better to do these doing right turns so as to avoid riding through intersections across traffic.

Workout Description: Warm up very thoroughly for at least 15 minutes. Begin riding the course. As you come out of each corner, stand and accelerate explosively for about 10 seconds. Sit and pedal easily until the next corner, where you will again jump and attack out of the corner. Repeat these short but intense efforts out of every corner for 15 minutes. Ride easily for 10 minutes, then repeat another 15 minutes of hard efforts. Warm down. Total workout length: 1 hour.

Chapter 8
Leg Strength Workouts

Cycling requires not only aerobic and anaerobic fitness; it is a sport that requires considerable leg strength. With every pedal stroke, you are pushing against the force of the pedal. The stronger you are, the easier it will be to push on the pedal at a given speed and cadence, allowing you to ride at a given pace with less effort. Or you will be able to ride with more force with each pedal stroke, thus allowing you to go faster. So whether your goal is to ride 100 miles or to race faster, the stronger you are, the better you will be able to reach your objective. Strength workouts occur year-round, although their nature varies depending on the season. The off-season is a good time to get to the gym and do some leg weight workouts. You may do up to 2 strength workouts a week in the gym. This will build base strength that is difficult to obtain just from riding. As the weather improves and you can ride your bike more, you will want to shift your leg strength workouts to your bike, such as various hill-climbing or large-gear workouts. You'll continue these, likely just once a week, during the main riding season. The workouts listed in this chapter focus primarily on the legs. It is strongly recommended that cyclists maintain an upper body strength program year-round as well. It's not that cyclists require a strong upper body, but this will help balance out their strength and work their upper body, which gets neglected if cycling is their only form of exercise. Strength training also helps prevent osteoporosis, and because cycling is not a weight-bearing exercise, some weight training should be added for your long-term health.

Please note: Be careful with any of these workouts, especially if you have knee or back problems and as you move to higher levels of resistance, to avoid injury. It is strongly advised that you get proper instruction on technique from a trained coach or personal trainer for these leg strength workouts.

Workout 53: Low RPM Seated Hill Climbs

Purpose of Workout: This workout builds leg strength on the bike. Often, riders do a lot of miles on the bike and build tremendous cardiovascular fitness but may lose some leg strength if specific strength workouts are not done during the cycling season. This workout is similar to doing leg presses, except it's done on the bike with hills providing the resistance. The intent is not to spin but to pedal at a deliberately slow cadence. The reason for this is to ensure that you are putting enough force on the pedals to elicit strength gains. At low RPMs, the force is greater than at higher RPMs.

Course Description: Find a hill that is at least a ½ mile long. It can be fairly moderate to quite steep. You will use your gears to determine the correct force and leg speed. You can either find a course with a number of hills or find a circuit that repeats the same hill over and over.

Workout Description: Warm up thoroughly for at least 15 minutes. Do this entire workout staying seated. As you approach the hill, select a fairly large gear that allows you to pedal up the hill at no more than 60 RPM. This will feel ridiculously slow if you are used to spinning. Do this entire hill interval while seated on your saddle. Do not be concerned with either your speed (it will be slow) or your heart rate, which won't be really high either. This is strictly a leg strength exercise. Repeat this interval several times, working up to a maximum of 10 times. Spin easily for 5 minutes between hill intervals. Cool down for 10 minutes. Total workout length: 1 hour.

Modification: If no suitable hill is available, you can also do these on a level road or a slight grade while riding into a strong headwind using a large gear.

Workout 54: Low RPM Standing Hill Climbs

Purpose of Workout: This workout is similar to Workout 53 with the exception that this is done standing, to develop standing leg strength. The intent is not to spin but to pedal at a deliberately slow cadence. The reason for this is to ensure that you are putting enough force on the pedals to elicit strength gains. At low RPMs, the force is greater than at higher RPMs.

Course Description: Find a hill that is at least a ½ mile long. It can be fairly moderate to quite steep. You will use your gears to determine the correct force and leg speed. You can either find a course with a number of hills or find a circuit that repeats the same hill over and over.

Workout Description: Warm up thoroughly for at least 15 minutes. As you approach the hill, select a fairly large gear that allows you to pedal up the hill at no more than 60 RPM while standing. This will feel ridiculously slow if you are used to spinning up hills. Do the entire hill interval staying standing. Focus on both pushing and pulling on the pedals as smoothly as possible. Do not be concerned with either your speed (it will be slow) or your heart rate, which won't be really high either. This is strictly a leg strength exercise. Repeat this interval several times, working up to a maximum of 10 times. Spin easily for 5 minutes between hill intervals. Cool down for 10 minutes. Total workout length: 1 hour.

Modification: If no suitable hill is available, you can also do these on a level road into a strong headwind using a large gear.

Workout 55: Large Gear Grinds

Purpose of Workout: The intent of this workout is to develop leg strength in the seated position. These intervals will be done at fairly low RPMs to maximize the force of each pedal stroke. This workout will be based on leg speed, not on heart rate, as this is a strength workout. However, your heart rate may get fairly high.

Course Description: These are best done on a fairly level road where you can keep your cadence constant. A course with up-and-down hills makes this workout difficult. If there is a wind, these intervals are preferably done into the wind. Doing intervals with a tailwind makes it difficult to maintain the force and low RPM required.

Workout Description: Warm up thoroughly for at least 15 minutes. Begin an interval by shifting into a large gear that you can only turn over at 60–70 RPMs. This should feel like a very slow cadence to you, but remember, you are focusing on high force, not high cadence. Hold this pace for the duration of the interval. Begin with 6-minute intervals and work up to 10 minutes. Spin in a low gear for 5 minutes then repeat another 6- to 10-minute large gear grind. Cool down for 10 minutes. Total workout length: 45 minutes.

Modification: You can also do this very effectively on a trainer, assuming your trainer provides great enough resistance to generate the force required to pedal at low RPMs.

Workout 56: Back Squats for Strength Endurance

Purpose of Workout: The intent of this workout is to develop leg strength for sustained power output. This is different from pure strength. It is about training your legs to put out moderately high force for a long period of time rather than the maximum force you can do 1 or a few times. Cycling is an endurance sport, and you need to do the pedaling motion thousands of times during a ride. Having more strength per pedal stroke will help you ride faster and tire less quickly. The muscles that are trained primarily are the gluteus maximus, hamstrings, and quadriceps, along with core muscles.

Equipment: You will need a barbell and squat rack to do these. You will also want to have a stationary bike or your bike on an indoor trainer available.

Workout Description: Warm up on your stationary bike for 10 minutes. You will want to start with a very low weight the first time you do these, perhaps even just with the empty bar. It will take your legs a couple of weeks to get used to the exercise. Select a weight for which you can complete 5 sets of 20 reps. Complete your first set, then get on your bike and spin for 5 minutes between sets. Spin for 10 minutes at the end. When you can complete 5 sets of 20, then it's time to increase the weight on the barbell. Increase it by the next incremental weight available. Total workout length: 55 minutes.

Exercise Description: Stand under the bar and rest the bar on your shoulders. Grab onto the bar at shoulder-width. Lift the bar and step back away from the rack. Keep your head tilted slightly up throughout the squat. Lower yourself by flexing the knees and hips while keeping your torso at a constant angle. Your hips should move down and back as if sitting on a chair. Stop flexing when 1 of 3 things occurs: 1) your heels come off the ground, 2) your thighs are parallel to the floor, or 3) your torso begins to round forward. Stop momentarily at the bottom of the motion and then extend the knees and hips and rise upward until standing erect. Pause momentarily before starting the next rep. Keep your back flat and elbows out throughout the exercise. Exhale as you stand up out of the squat. Focus on keeping your core muscles engaged throughout the squat.

Modification: You may hold 2 dumbbells in place of using a barbell if you don't have a squat rack available. See Workout 57 for doing these on a leg press machine.

Workout 57: Leg Presses
for Strength Endurance

Purpose of Workout: The intent of this workout is to develop leg strength for sustained power output. This is different from pure strength. It is about training your legs to put out force for a long period of time rather than the maximum force you can do at one time. Cycling is an endurance sport, and you need to do the pedaling motion thousands of times during a ride. Having more strength per pedal stroke will help you ride faster and tire less quickly. The muscles that are trained primarily are the gluteus maximus, hamstrings, and quadriceps.

Equipment: You will need a leg press or hip sled machine to do this workout. You will also want to have a stationary bike or your bike on an indoor trainer available.

Workout Description: Warm up on your indoor bike for 10 minutes. You will want to start with a very low weight the first few times you do these. It will take your legs a couple of weeks to get used to the exercise. Do 20 reps of leg presses per set. Get on your bike and spin for 5 minutes between sets. Work your way up to a total of 5 sets. Spin for 10 minutes at the end. When you can complete 5 sets of 20 reps, increase the weight. Total workout length: 55 minutes.

Exercise Description: Sit on the machine with your back against the seat pad. Place your feet on the platform at hip-width, with the toes as high as or slightly higher than your knees in the lowest position. At the lowest position, your knees should be parallel to the platform. Start by extending your knees and hips to push you away from the platform. Exhale while pushing to a fully extended position, but do not lock your knees. Pause momentarily, then flex your knees and hips and come back to the beginning position. Pause momentarily before starting the next rep.

Modification: See Workout 56 to do these with squats.

Workout 58: Back Squats for Maximum Strength

Purpose of Workout: The intent of this workout is to develop maximum leg strength. This is about developing pure strength in your leg muscles. This will help you climb hills, attack, and sprint more effectively. Having more strength per pedal stroke will help you ride faster and tire less quickly. The muscles that are trained primarily are the gluteus maximus, hamstrings, and quadriceps, along with core muscles.

Equipment: You will need a barbell and squat rack to do these. You will also want to have a stationary bike or your bike on an indoor trainer available.

Workout Description: Warm up on your stationary bike for 10 minutes. You should only do these squats after you have been doing strength endurance squats (see Workout 56) for several weeks as this weight will be quite heavy and you will need to have developed a strong foundation first. Select a weight that you can just barely lift for 6 reps. Do 6 reps of squats per set. Get on your bike and spin for 5 minutes between sets. Work your way up to a total of 5 sets. Spin for 10 minutes at the end. Total workout length: 50 minutes.

Exercise Description: Stand under the bar and rest the bar on your shoulders. Grab onto the bar at shoulder-width. Lift the bar and step away from the rack. Keep your head tilted slightly up throughout the squat. Lower yourself by flexing the knees and hips while keeping your torso at a constant angle. Your hips should move down and back as if sitting on a chair. Stop flexing when 1 of 3 things occurs: 1) your heels come off the ground, 2) your thighs are parallel to the floor, or 3) your torso begins to round forward. Stop momentarily and then extend the knees and hips and rise upward until standing erect. Pause momentarily before starting the next rep. Exhale as you stand up out of the squat. Focus on keeping your core muscles engaged throughout the squat. Keep your back flat and elbows out throughout the exercise.

Modification: See Workout 59 for doing these on a leg press machine.

Workout 59: Leg Presses for Maximum Strength

Purpose of Workout: The intent of this workout is to develop maximum leg strength. This is about developing pure strength in your leg muscles. This will help you climb hills, attack, and sprint more effectively. Having more strength per pedal stroke will help you ride faster and tire less quickly. The muscles that are trained primarily are the gluteus maximus, hamstrings, and quadriceps, along with core muscles.

Equipment: You will need a leg press or hip sled machine to do this workout. You will also want to have a stationary bike or your bike on an indoor trainer available.

Workout Description: Warm up on your stationary bike for 10 minutes. You should only do these leg presses after you have been doing strength endurance leg presses (see Workout 57) for several weeks as this weight will be quite heavy and you will need to have developed a strong foundation first. Select a weight that you can just barely lift for 6 reps. Do 6 reps of leg presses per set. Get on your bike and spin for 5 minutes between sets. Work your way up to a total of 5 sets. Spin for 10 minutes at the end. Total workout length: 50 minutes.

Exercise Description: Sit on the machine with your back against the seat pad. Place your feet on the platform at hip-width, with the toes as high as or slightly higher than your knees in the lowest position. At the lowest position, your knees should be parallel to the platform. Start by extending your knees and hips to push you away from the platform. Exhale while pushing to a fully extended position, but do not lock your knees. Pause momentarily, then flex your knees and hips and come back to the beginning position. Pause momentarily before starting the next rep.

Modification: See Workout 58 to do these using squats.

Workout 60: Box Squats

Purpose of Workout: The intent of this workout is to develop explosive leg strength and power. The box squat requires an explosive force when rising up out of the squat from a stationary position on the box. This will help you jump, attack, and sprint more effectively. One advantage of the box squat over the back squat is that it takes away any concern about squatting too low. You will squat to the height of the box every time—just be sure the box is the right height for you. Another advantage is that you will find that your hamstring muscles are not as sore as with regular back squats. The muscles that are trained primarily are the gluteus maximus, hamstrings, and quadriceps, along with core muscles.

Equipment: You will need a barbell and squat rack, and a sturdy box or bench to do this workout. The box or bench should be of a height that allows your thighs to be parallel to the floor when you are sitting on it. You will also want to have a stationary bike or your bike on an indoor trainer available.

Workout Description: Warm up on your stationary bike for 10 minutes. Select a weight that you can just lift for 15 reps. Do 15 reps of squats per set. Get on your bike and spin for 5 minutes between sets. Work your way up to a total of 4 sets. Spin for 10 minutes at the end. Total workout length: 55 minutes.

Exercise Description: Stand under the bar and rest the bar on your shoulders. Grab onto the bar at shoulder-width. Lift the bar and step away from the rack. Keep your head tilted slightly up throughout the squat. Lower yourself by flexing the knees and hips while keeping your torso at a constant angle. Your hips should move down and back as if sitting on a chair. Lower yourself down onto the box or bench but avoid dropping yourself onto it. Sit on the box momentarily and relax your hip flexor muscles. Then lean forward slightly and explosively extend the knees and hips and rise upward until standing erect. Pause momentarily before starting the next rep. Exhale as you stand up out of the squat. Focus on keeping your core muscles engaged throughout the squat. Keep your back flat and elbows out throughout the exercise.

Modification: You can also do these holding 2 dumbbells instead of a barbell.

Workout 61: One-Legged Squats

Purpose of Workout: The intent of this workout is to develop leg strength for sustained power output, to ensure each leg is developing strength equally, and also to improve your balance. Cycling is an endurance sport, and you need to do the pedaling motion thousands of times during a ride. Having more strength per pedal stroke will help you ride faster and tire less quickly. The muscles that are trained primarily are the gluteus maximus, hamstrings, and quadriceps, along with core muscles. In addition, cycling is a one-legged activity; you pedal with one leg at a time. This is one of the exercises that isolate each leg separately. This is also a great exercise to do for leg strength training when you are traveling and don't have access to a gym.

Equipment: You only need yourself to do this exercise. It is best to have a stationary bike or your bike on an indoor trainer available.

Workout Description: Warm up on your stationary bike for 10 minutes. Do 10 squats with one leg, then switch and do 10 reps with the other leg. Complete your first set, then get on your bike and spin for 5 minutes between sets. Work your way up to 5 sets of 10 reps. Spin for 10 minutes at the end. Total workout length: 55 minutes.

Exercise Description: Stand on one leg with the other leg held out in front of you. Hold your arms out in front of you for balance. Flex your hip and knee and try to lower yourself down to the point where your thigh is parallel to the ground. Stop momentarily and then extend the knee and hip and rise upward until standing erect. Pause momentarily before starting the next rep. Keep your back flat throughout the exercise. Exhale as you stand up out of the squat. Focus on keeping your core muscles engaged throughout the squat. This is a very difficult exercise, so don't be surprised if you can't do it.

Modifications: At first you may not be able to do even 1 rep. There are 3 modifications to this exercise from which you may choose until you become strong enough to do them unassisted.

1) Hold on to a table, desk, or some other solid object with one hand as you lower yourself down. You may also need to assist yourself by pushing with your hand to raise yourself back up, as well as to balance.

2) A second way to assist yourself is to do these while sitting down onto a chair. You'll find that even if you can't do these unassisted, you should be able to do these when sitting onto and out of a chair.

3) A third way to make these easier is to do these with the unweighted knee bent with the foot held behind your body rather than in front. This makes it easier to balance and to bend down lower than with the leg out in front.

If you want to make this more difficult yet, do these while holding dumbbells.

Workout 62: Split Squats

Purpose of Workout: The intent of this workout is to develop leg strength for sustained power output, to ensure each leg is developing strength equally, and also to improve your balance. Cycling is an endurance sport, and you need to do the pedaling motion thousands of times during a ride. Having more strength per pedal stroke will help you ride faster and tire less quickly. The muscles that are trained primarily are the gluteus maximus, hamstrings, and quadriceps, along with core muscles. In addition, cycling is a one-legged activity; you pedal with one leg at a time. This is one of the exercises that isolate each leg separately. This is a great exercise to do for leg strength training when you are traveling and don't have access to a gym. This exercise is easier than lunges (Workout 65) but works the same muscles, so if you have trouble doing lunges, do split squats instead.

Equipment: You only need yourself to do this exercise. However, for more advanced lifting, you can use dumbbells or a barbell for added resistance. It is best to have a stationary bike or your bike on an indoor trainer available.

Workout Description: Warm up on your stationary bike for 10 minutes. Do 10 split squats with one leg, then switch and do 10 reps with the other leg. Complete your first set, then get on your bike and spin for 5 minutes between sets. Work your way up to 5 sets of 10 reps. Spin for 10 minutes at the end. Total workout length: 55 minutes.

Exercise Description: Start by taking a big step forward with one leg, placing the front foot flat on the ground. The rear foot will be flexed, and you will be on your toes. Bend your knees and hips, dropping your buttocks towards the ground. Continue bending until your forward leg has a 90 degree bend at the knee and your rear knee is 1 to 2 inches off the ground. Be sure that when you are in the lowest position your front knee does not extend in front of your toes. If it does, you need to take a bigger step forward before starting. Pause momentarily, then push upwards and extend the knees and hips back to the starting position, keeping the feet stationary on the ground. Pause momentarily before starting the next rep. Keep your head looking forward, not down, and keep your back flat throughout the exercise. Exhale as you stand up out of the squat. Focus on keeping your core muscles engaged throughout the squat.

Modifications: There are a number of ways to increase the challenge of this beyond just using your body weight.

1) Hold onto dumbbells for added weight.

2) Hold a weighted barbell on your shoulders as you would with squats while doing these.

3) Hold a medicine ball out in front of you with your arms extended for additional resistance and core stability.

Workout 63: Bulgarian Split Squats

Purpose of Workout: The intent of this workout is to develop leg strength for sustained power output, to ensure each leg is developing strength equally, and also to improve your balance. Cycling is an endurance sport, and you need to do the pedaling motion thousands of times during a ride. Having more strength per pedal stroke will help you ride faster and tire less quickly. The muscles that are trained primarily are the gluteus maximus, hamstrings, and quadriceps, along with core muscles. This exercise is similar to the split squat (Workout 62) with the difference being that the back foot is raised up on a bench. This increases the need for balance and stretches the quadriceps of the rear leg. In addition, cycling is a one-legged activity; you pedal with one leg at a time. This is one of the exercises that isolate each leg separately. This is a great exercise to do for leg strength training when you are traveling and don't have access to a gym.

Equipment: You only need yourself and a bench or chair to do this exercise. However, for more advanced lifting, you can use dumbbells or a barbell for added weight. It is best to have a stationary bike or your bike on an indoor trainer available.

Workout Description: Warm up on your stationary bike for 10 minutes. Do 10 Bulgarian split squats with one leg, then switch and do 10 reps with the other leg. Complete your first set, then get on your bike and spin for 5 minutes between sets. Work your way up to 5 sets of 10 reps. Spin for 10 minutes at the end. Total workout length: 55 minutes.

Exercise Description: Start by placing the toes of your back foot onto a bench. The bench should be slightly lower than knee height. Your front foot is placed out in front of you. Proceed into a squat position by bending your knees and lowering your hips downward. Continue downward until your forward thigh is parallel to the ground. Be sure that when you are in the lowest position your front knee does not extend in front of your toes. If it does, you need to take a bigger step forward before starting. Stop momentarily and then extend the knees and hips and rise upward until standing erect. Pause momentarily before starting the next rep. Keep your head looking forward, not down, and keep your back flat throughout the exercise. Exhale as you stand up out of the squat. Focus on keeping your core muscles engaged throughout the squat.

Modifications: There are a number of ways to increase the challenge of this beyond just using your body weight.

1) Hold onto dumbbells for added weight.

2) Hold a weighted barbell on your shoulders as you would with squats while doing these.

3) Hold a medicine ball out in front of you with your arms extended for additional resistance and core stability.

Workout 64: Step-Ups

<u>**Purpose of Workout:**</u> The intent of this workout is to develop leg strength for sustained power output, to ensure each leg is developing strength equally, and also to improve your balance. Cycling is an endurance sport, and you need to do the pedaling motion thousands of times during a ride. Having more strength per pedal stroke will help you ride faster and tire less quickly. The muscles that are trained primarily are the gluteus maximus, hamstrings, and quadriceps, along with core muscles. In addition, cycling is a one-legged activity; you pedal with one leg at a time. This is one of the exercises that isolate each leg separately. This is a great exercise to do for leg strength training when you are traveling and don't have access to a gym.

<u>**Equipment:**</u> You only need yourself and a sturdy box or bench to step up onto to do this exercise. However, for more advanced lifting, you can use dumbbells or a barbell for added weight. It is best to have a stationary bike or your bike on an indoor trainer available.

<u>**Workout Description:**</u> Warm up on your stationary bike for 10 minutes. Do 20 step-ups with one leg, then switch and do 20 reps with the other leg. Complete your first set, then get on your bike and spin for 5 minutes between sets. Work your way up to 5 sets of 20 reps. Spin for 10 minutes at the end. Total workout length: 55 minutes.

<u>**Exercise Description:**</u> Start by placing your left foot onto a box or bench with the right foot to the right of the box or bench. The height of the box or bench needs to be of the correct height for you. When your foot is on it, your knee should be at a 90 degree bend. Place your weight on the left foot. Step up with your left leg, keeping the torso erect (don't lean forward). *Lift* your right foot off the ground but resist pushing off or hopping up with it. This is very important and will take some practice, but you will notice how much harder it works the left leg when you do it correctly. To help do this correctly, stand on your right heel. This will prevent you from pushing off with your toes. At the highest position, stand erect and pause momentarily. Then step

back down, keeping the weight on the left foot until the right foot touches the ground. When the right foot touches the ground, repeat the exercise. Keep your head looking forward, not down, and keep your torso erect throughout the exercise. Exhale as you stand up on the box/bench. Focus on keeping your core muscles engaged throughout the step-up. Once you complete a set with the left leg, do a set with the right leg.

Modifications: There are a number of ways to increase the challenge of this beyond just using your body weight.

1) Hold onto dumbbells for added weight.

2) Hold a weighted barbell on your shoulders as you would with squats while doing these.

3) Hold a medicine ball out in front of you or overhead with your arms extended for additional resistance and core stability.

Workout 65: Forward Lunges

Purpose of Workout: The intent of this workout is to develop leg strength for sustained power output, to ensure each leg is developing strength equally, and also to improve your balance. Cycling is an endurance sport, and you need to do the pedaling motion thousands of times during a ride. Having more strength per pedal stroke will help you ride faster and tire less quickly. The lunge is a very popular and excellent exercise for leg strength and balance. The muscles that are trained primarily are the gluteus maximus, hamstrings, and quadriceps, along with core muscles. The lunge has the additional plyometric component, which most of the other leg strength exercises in this chapter do not have. When standing up out of the lunge, an explosive contraction of your quadriceps muscles is required. In addition, cycling is a one-legged activity; you pedal with one leg at a time. This is one of the exercises that isolate each leg separately. This is a great exercise to do for leg strength training when you are traveling and don't have access to a gym.

Equipment: You only need yourself to do this exercise. However, for more advanced lifting, you can use dumbbells, a medicine ball, or a barbell for added weight. It is best to have a stationary bike or your bike on an indoor trainer available.

Workout Description: Warm up on your stationary bike for 10 minutes. Do 20 lunges with one leg, then switch and do 20 reps with the other leg. Complete your first set, then get on your bike and spin for 5 minutes between sets. Work your way up to 5 sets of 20 reps. Spin for 10 minutes at the end. Total workout length: 55 minutes.

Exercise Description: Start by taking a big step forward with one leg, placing the front foot flat on the ground. The rear knee will begin to flex a little. Bend your lead knee and hip, keeping your knee in line with your foot, and allow your rear knee to flex. Continue until your forward leg has a 90 degree bend at the knee and your rear knee is 1 to 2 inches off the ground. Your rear foot will roll up on your toes. Be sure that when you are in the lowest position your front knee does not extend in front of your toes. If it does, you need to take a bigger step forward before starting. Pause momentarily, then push upwards and backwards explosively and extend the forward knee and hip back to the starting position with your feet together. Pause momentarily before starting the next rep. Keep your head looking forward, not down, and maintain an erect torso throughout the exercise. Exhale as you push back out of the lunge. Focus on keeping your core muscles engaged throughout the exercise.

Modifications: There are a number of ways to increase the challenge of this beyond just using your body weight.

1) Hold onto dumbbells for added weight.

2) Hold a weighted barbell on your shoulders as you would with squats while doing these.

3) Hold a medicine ball out in front of you or overhead with your arms extended for additional resistance and core stability.

Workout 66: Reverse Lunges

Purpose of Workout: The intent of this workout is to develop leg strength for sustained power output, to ensure each leg is developing strength equally, and also to improve your balance. Cycling is an endurance sport, and you need to do the pedaling motion thousands of times during a ride. Having more strength per pedal stroke will help you ride faster and tire less quickly. The lunge is a very popular and excellent exercise for leg strength and balance. The muscles that are trained primarily are the gluteus maximus, hamstrings, and quadriceps, along with core muscles. In addition, cycling is a one-legged activity; you pedal with one leg at a time. This is one of the exercises that isolate each leg separately. This is a great exercise to do for leg strength training when you are traveling and don't have access to a gym.

Equipment: You only need yourself to do this exercise. However, for more advanced lifting, you can use dumbbells, a medicine ball, or a barbell for added weight. It is best to have a stationary bike or your bike on an indoor trainer available.

Workout Description: Warm up on your stationary bike for 10 minutes. Do 20 lunges with one leg, then switch and do 20 reps with the other leg. Complete your first set, then get on your bike and spin for 5 minutes between sets. Work your way up to 5 sets of 20 reps. Spin for 10 minutes at the end. Total workout length: 55 minutes.

Exercise Description: Start by taking a big step backwards with one leg, placing the foot on the ground behind you and lowering yourself down by dropping your rear knee and flexing your forward knee. Control the speed with your forward leg. Continue until your forward leg has a 90 degree bend at the knee and your rear knee is 1 to 2 inches off the ground. Be sure that when you are in the lowest position your front knee does not extend in front of your toes. If it does, you need to take a bigger step backward before starting. Pause momentarily and then lift upwards with the front leg and bring the rear leg forward to the starting position. Avoid pushing off with the rear foot; rather, think about lifting up with the front leg. It's actually the front leg you are working with reverse lunges. Pause momentarily before starting the next rep. Keep your head looking forward, not down, and maintain an erect torso throughout the exercise. Exhale as you push forward out of the lunge. Focus on keeping your core muscles engaged throughout the exercise.

Modifications: There are a number of ways to increase the challenge of this beyond just using your body weight.

1) Hold onto dumbbells for added weight.

2) Hold a weighted barbell on your shoulders as you would with squats while doing these.

3) Hold a medicine ball out in front of you or overhead with your arms extended for additional resistance and core stability.

Workout 67: Jump Squats

Purpose of Workout: The intent of this workout is to develop explosive leg strength for power output. This is a plyometric exercise and requires powerful, explosive jumping. The muscles that are trained primarily are the gluteus maximus, hamstrings, and quadriceps, along with core muscles. It will also cause your heart rate to rise quite rapidly as it is also an anaerobic exercise. This is a great exercise to do for leg strength training when you are traveling and don't have access to a gym.

Equipment: You only need yourself to do this exercise. It is best to have a stationary bike or your bike on an indoor trainer for warming up and cooling down.

Workout Description: Warm up on your stationary bike for 10 minutes. Do 20 jump squats. Rest for 2 minutes and then repeat another set of 20 reps. Work your way up to 5 sets of 20 reps. Spin for 10 minutes at the end. Total workout length: 35 minutes.

Exercise Description: Start by standing with feet at shoulder-width. Arms should be flexed at the elbows. Bend the knees so that the thighs are parallel to the ground and flex your torso slightly forward. Explode vertically and swing your arms up over your head to drive yourself upward. Land back on both feet and quickly repeat 20 reps. You do not want to pause between jumps but rather explode back up as soon as you finish the last rep. Extend your ankles with each jump. Keep your head looking forward, not looking down. Exhale as you jump. Focus on keeping your core muscles engaged throughout the exercise.

Modification: You can also do this by starting in the split squat position (see Workout 62) and jumping up and landing with one foot out in front and the other in back—the jump split-squat. This requires more force from the forward leg and more balance as well.

Workout 68: Deadlift

Purpose of Workout: The intent of this workout is to develop maximum leg strength. This is about developing pure strength in your leg and gluteus maximus muscles. This will help you develop more force. Being able to apply more force per pedal stroke will help you ride faster and tire less quickly. The muscles that are trained primarily are the gluteus maximus, hamstrings, and quadriceps, along with core and especially back muscles.

Equipment: You will need a barbell to do this exercise. You will also want to have a stationary bike or your bike on an indoor trainer available.

Workout Description: Warm up on your stationary bike for 10 minutes. You should only do these squats after you have developed a strong core and leg strength foundation first. Select a weight that you can just barely lift for 10 reps. Do 10 reps of squats per set. Get on your bike and spin for 5 minutes between sets. Work your way up to a total of 4 sets. Spin for 10 minutes at the end. Total workout length: 45 minutes.

Exercise Description: Stand with feet about shoulder-width apart. Squat down and grab the barbell on the floor. Grab the bar with your hands slightly wider than shoulder-width, outside of the knees, with elbows extended. Lift the bar by extending the hips and knees. Keep the bar close to your shins as you lift it. Stand up fully erect. Then flex the knees and hips and lower the bar back to the ground, without curving your torso. Keep your head facing forward or slightly upward and maintain a flat back throughout the exercise. Exhale as you stand and pull the bar up. Focus on keeping your core muscles engaged throughout the squat. Pause momentarily before starting the next rep.

Workout 69: Leg (Hamstring) Curls

Purpose of Workout: The intent of this workout is to develop maximum leg strength, specifically of the hamstring muscles. This exercise specifically helps improve strength in the pedal stroke when you are pulling back and up with the foot at the bottom of the pedal stroke. Many of the leg strengthening workouts focus on the quadriceps in the front of the leg. This exercise will help maintain balance in the opposing muscles.

Equipment: You will need a leg curl machine to do this workout. You will also want to have a stationary bike or your bike on an indoor trainer available.

Workout Description: Warm up on your stationary bike for 10 minutes. During the strength endurance phase, select a weight that allows you to do 20 reps per set. During the maximum strength phase, select a weight that allows you to do 6 reps per set. Do 1 set and then get on your bike and spin for 5 minutes between sets. Do a total of 5 sets. Spin for 10 minutes at the end. Total workout length: 50 minutes.

Exercise Description: Sit or lie on the leg curl machine, depending on the style. Place the ankles behind the foot roller pad. Align the knees with the axis of the machine. Adjust the machine if necessary. Grab the handles. Flex the knees and pull back on the pad behind your ankles. Avoid letting the thighs or hips come off the pad. Pull back until the knees are at least at a 90 degree bend. Pause briefly then extend the knees and straighten the legs. Do not lock the knees at the end of the motion.

Modification: The hamstrings can also be worked using rubber exercise bands if a leg curl machine is not available.

Workout 70: Leg Extensions

Purpose of Workout: The intent of this workout is to develop maximum leg strength, specifically of the quadriceps muscles. This exercise helps improve strength for the over-the-top and downward push of the pedal stroke as the knee extends. There is some debate as to whether the leg extension exercise is useful for many athletes, but in cycling, leg extension is a major component of the pedal stroke. Why do you think cyclists have such well-defined quads? By the way, if you don't consciously try to push the pedal over the top of the stroke (the 10 to 2 o'clock position), try it; it will smooth out and strengthen your pedal stroke.

Equipment: You will need a leg extension machine to do this workout. You will also want to have a stationary bike or your bike on an indoor trainer available.

Workout Description: Warm up on your stationary bike for 10 minutes. During the strength endurance phase, select a weight that allows you to do 20 reps per set. During the maximum strength phase, select a weight that allows you to do 6 reps per set. Do 1 set and then get on your bike and spin for 5 minutes between sets. Do a total of 5 sets. Spin for 10 minutes at the end. Total workout length: 50 minutes.

Exercise Description: Sit on the leg extension machine. Place the ankles behind the foot roller pad. Align the knees with the axis of the machine. Adjust the machine if necessary. Grab the handles. Push up on the pad by extending the knees. Keep your back and hips pressed against the pad throughout the motion. Extend the knees but do not straighten out the legs fully. Maintain about a 20 degree slight bend in the knees. Pause briefly then slowly flex the knees and bend the legs back to the starting position.

Modification: The quads can also be worked using rubber exercise bands if a leg curl machine is not available.

Workout 71: Calf Raises

Purpose of Workout: The intent of this workout is to develop calf strength. This exercise helps improve foot stability through the pedal stroke by developing a stronger calf. It may also help your power by providing a small push on the pedals at the bottom of the pedal stroke.

Equipment: All you need for this exercise is a raised object that you can stand on such as an exercise step, or if you don't have that, a stair or curb will suffice.

Exercise Description: Warm up on your stationary bike for 10 minutes. Stand on the toes of your left foot on the object. Bend the right leg up behind you. Allow your left heel to drop down a few inches below your toes. Slowly raise yourself up onto your toes as high as you can then lower yourself back down. Work up to 3 sets of 20 reps of these. Rest briefly between sets. Repeat with the right foot. This exercise can be done in conjunction with other leg strength exercises. Total workout length: 20 minutes.

Modification: Hold dumbbells or a medicine ball in your hands or a barbell across your shoulders as you do this for added weight and balance.

Workout 72: Core Strengthening

Purpose of Workout: The core muscles, those of the abdominals, back, and hips, are critical in transmitting your power to the pedals. The legs push and pull off the hips, which need to be held steady by the core muscles to provide efficient transfer of power. If your hips rock and your back wobbles back and forth during your pedal stroke, you are wasting energy. Working to develop strong core strength should be done year-round to make your cycling more efficient.

Equipment: While there is variety of equipment that can be used to increase core strength, the exercises listed here only require your own body weight, and perhaps an exercise mat if desired.

Workout Description: Core exercises can be done almost every day. Try to do them at least 3 times per week. You only need to do 1 set of each exercise per day.

Exercise Descriptions:

Plank: Facing down on the floor, raise yourself up on your forearms with your elbows bent at 90 degree angles. Rise up on your toes. Maintain a straight line with your torso between your head and your feet. Hold this position as long as you can, working up to 1 minute.

Superman: Lying facedown on the floor with your legs extended back and your arms extended out in front of your head, simultaneously raise your right arm and left leg. Hold this for 1 second then lower back down and repeat with the other arm and leg. Avoid raising your head as you raise your arms. Shoulders and hips should remain as still as possible during movements. Repeat this as many times as you can, working up to 40 reps.

Back Plank: Lying on your back, raise yourself up on your elbows underneath your body and on your heels. Maintain a straight line with your torso between your head and your feet. Hold this position as long as you can, working up to 1 minute. Avoid looking down at your feet; rather, look up towards the ceiling.

<u>Single Leg Good Mornings:</u> Start by standing erect, holding a barbell or broomstick on your shoulders behind your head. Kick one leg back, keeping the front knee straight, and bend forward at the waist. Bend over until your upper body and extended leg are parallel to the floor, or as far as your flexibility allows. Return to the upright position and repeat with the other leg. Do as many reps as you can, working up to 40 reps with each leg.

<u>Side Plank:</u> Lying on your right side, raise yourself up onto your right elbow and on your right foot. Place your left hand on your hip. Maintain a straight line from your head to your feet. Hold this position as long as you can, working up to 1 minute. Repeat on your left side.

<u>Bicycle Crunches:</u> Lying on your back, place your hands on the side of your head near your ears. Raise your legs up and bend them 90 degrees at the knees and hips. Curl your right shoulder and left knee towards each other until your elbow and knee touch. Lower them down to the starting position and repeat with the left elbow and right knee. Repeat 40 times with both arms/legs.

Modification: Try a Pilates class. Pilates is great for increasing core strength, stability, and flexibility, as well as overall body awareness.

Chapter 9
Leg Speed Workouts

If you've watched accomplished cyclists ride, you undoubtedly have noticed how smooth and effortless their pedal strokes seem. This is because they have developed a very fluid pedal stroke from years of riding. The French call it "supplesse." But more important than looking nice, it serves a very useful function. The smoother your pedal stroke, the more efficient you are, resulting in riding longer or harder with less effort. It also results in being able to ride more smoothly, making it easier for you to maintain a steady pace, a skill essential if drafting closely behind other riders in a pack. It also makes it easier for those behind you to draft behind you. A fluid leg stroke doesn't just happen. There are leg drills that can help develop this technique, and these are included in this chapter. These workouts do not require a lot of leg strength, so these can be done on your easy days or added in to your endurance rides or done as part of your warm-up. You should try to do at least 1 of these workouts each week throughout the year.

Workout 73: Single Leg Spinning

Purpose of Workout: This workout develops your pedal stroke smoothness. Cyclists do not push on the pedal uniformly throughout the pedal stroke. You are strongest on the downstroke (2 to 6 o'clock position) and weaker on the rest of the stroke. However, because one leg is pushing down while the other comes up, it tends to smooth out the stroke quite well. But, the smoothness of your pedal stroke can be improved by improving your ability to pedal in circles better throughout the entire stroke. This exercise will help you with this. It trains your muscles and neuromuscular system to work all the way around the pedal stroke rather than resting on the upstroke.

Course Description: You will need to have either toe clips or a clipless pedal system as you will need to be able to pull up on the pedals. This workout is best done on an indoor trainer as you will need to pull a foot out of your pedal and place it somewhere, and your trainer is a good place to rest it. If you can't do it on a trainer, you can do it outside, but you need to be careful with the non-spinning foot to keep it away from your back wheel, and you will have to balance yourself with one foot dangling to the side while you concentrate on pedaling with the other foot. You can also try this on rollers if you are accomplished at roller riding, although it brings the added complication of staying balanced on the rollers while you hold a foot to the side and pedal with the other. But if you can do it, it demonstrates that you have very good balance and is also something to do to impress your buddies!

Workout Description: Following a 10-minute warm-up, take 1 foot off of your pedal and place it in back on the trainer or hang it off to the side, being careful not to get it near the rear wheel. Select a gear that allows you to pedal about 80 RPM. Begin spinning with 1 leg, focusing on maintaining constant and uniform pressure to the pedals all the way around. You will consciously have to pay attention to pulling back at the bottom of the stroke, up on the upstroke, and over the top of the stroke. At first your pedal stroke will be jerky, especially as your leg gets tired, but with concentration and practice, it will smooth out. It will take some time though to see improvement. Try to pedal for a minute at first, although this may not even be possible. Then switch and do the other leg. Alternate legs, working up to 3 2-minute segments per leg. Total workout length: 20–25 minutes.

Modifications: This can also be done in combination with another workout, such as during a recovery ride or as a warm-up before you begin other intervals on your trainer.

Workout 74: Spin Accelerations

Purpose of Workout: This workout forces you to concentrate on applying uniform pressure to your pedals all the way around the pedal stroke. This exercise has you increase your cadence from about 80 up to your maximum cadence. It trains you to pedal smoothly across a range of leg speeds, and by accelerating your cadence, it allows you to think about applying a constant pressure to the pedals throughout the pedal stroke. It also allows you to identify your maximum cadence, which is the point right before you start bouncing on your saddle. Over time you should be able to increase your maximum cadence by developing smoother circles with your feet.

Course Description: This can be done on a level road or is great to do on an indoor trainer, especially rollers. Rollers will magnify any unevenness of your pedal stroke, and the bike will begin bouncing on the rollers when you've reached your maximum cadence. Initially do this on a stationary trainer until you have mastered doing these intervals smoothly. If done on the road, select a stretch of road that is level and ride in the direction of the tailwind. This workout focuses on technique not power, so you don't want resistance. A cadence monitor on your bike will be helpful for this workout.

Workout Description: Following a 10-minute warm-up, select a moderately low gear (e.g., 39 x 15). Begin the interval by accelerating from 80 RPM all the way up to your maximum cadence. Your maximum cadence is determined by the point at which you begin bouncing on your saddle. Once you begin bouncing, really focus on making nice round, smooth pedal strokes, and you should be able to reduce your tendency to bounce with practice. The total length of the interval is only 30 seconds. It should take you around 15 seconds to work up to your maximum cadence, and then hold it for the other 15 seconds. Ride easily for 3 minutes between intervals. Work your way up to 10 intervals. Total workout length: 50 minutes.

Modifications: This can also be done in combination with another workout, such as during a recovery ride or before you begin other intervals on your trainer. You don't need to do all 10 reps, but throw 1 or 2 in from time to time while out on rides, including endurance rides.

Workout 75: High Speed Spinning

Purpose of Workout: This workout forces you to concentrate on applying uniform pressure to your pedals all the way around the pedal stroke. This workout has you sustain a very high cadence to make spinning quickly feel more natural to you. This exercise is really more about training your neuromuscular system than your aerobic system. It's about technique. Over time you will be able to increase the cadence you can sustain without bouncing.

Course Description: This can be done on a level road or is great to do on an indoor trainer, especially rollers. Rollers will magnify any unevenness of your pedal stroke, and the bike will begin bouncing on the rollers when you've reached your maximum cadence. Initially do this on a stationary trainer until you have mastered doing these intervals smoothly. If done on the road, select a stretch of road that is level and ride in the direction of the tailwind. This workout focuses on technique not power, so you don't want resistance. A cadence monitor on your bike will be helpful for this workout.

Workout Description: Following a 10-minute warm-up, select a moderately low gear (e.g., 39 x 15). Begin the interval by accelerating quickly up to your maximum cadence. Your maximum cadence is determined by the point at which you begin bouncing on your saddle. Once you begin bouncing, really focus on making nice round, smooth pedal strokes, and you should be able to reduce your tendency to bounce. Hold this high cadence for 1 minute. Ride easily for 3 minutes between intervals. Work your way up to 6 intervals with practice. Total workout length: 35 minutes.

Modifications: This can also be done in combination with another workout, such as during a recovery ride or before you begin other intervals on your trainer. You don't need to do all 6 reps, but throw 1 or 2 in from time to time while out on rides, including endurance rides.

Workout 76: Downhill Spinning

Purpose of Workout: This workout trains you to increase and hold a high cadence. You should focus on spinning in nice, round circles with your feet and avoid bouncing in your saddle. Think about fluid feet. This workout will help you feel more comfortable at high RPMs and trains primarily your neuromuscular system, not your aerobic system. It's a technique drill.

Course Description: This needs to be done on downhills, to allow you to get up to a very high cadence. The hills work best when mildly downhill (great for learning this workout), but this exercise can be done on any steepness and length of hill. However, avoid extremely steep hills as they will be impossible to hold your spin. It's best just to select a hilly route and let the hills dictate the workout. Try to find a course with at least 8 to 10 downhills, or select a loop with 1 hill and repeat it several times.

Workout Description: Head out on your hilly course. As you approach the top of a hill, select a gear you think you can spin all the way to the bottom (this will take some practice) and start pedaling as you head downhill. Don't apply much pressure to the pedals, just focus on having your feet keep up with the pedals as the pedals accelerate. As your leg speed increases, focus on maintaining constant pressure to the pedals all the way around the pedal stroke. This will help you keep from bouncing. You should actually feel your buttocks lift off the saddle as your legs go faster and faster. If the hill becomes too steep and you find yourself bouncing, then shift to the next larger gear and try to resume spinning. Recover until the next downhill. Total workout length: 30–60 minutes.

Modifications: These downhill spin intervals can also be done in combination with another workout, such as during a recovery ride or endurance ride.

Workout 77: Sustained Spinning

Purpose of Workout: This workout forces you to concentrate on applying uniform pressure to your pedals all the way around the pedal stroke. This workout is about training your legs to spin at a high cadence for fairly long periods of time to make spinning seem more natural to you.

Course Description: This can be done on a level road or is great to do on an indoor trainer, especially rollers. Rollers will magnify any unevenness of your pedal stroke, and the bike will begin bouncing on the rollers when you've reached your maximum cadence. Initially do this on a stationary trainer until you have mastered doing these intervals smoothly. If done on the road, select a stretch of road that is level and ride in the direction of the tailwind. This workout focuses on technique not power, so you don't want resistance. A cadence monitor on your bike will be helpful for this workout.

Workout Description: Following a 10-minute warm-up, select a moderately low gear (e.g., 39 x 15). Begin the interval by accelerating up to a cadence about 10–15 RPMs above your normal cadence. Hold this cadence for 5 minutes at a time. It will take concentration and feel unnatural at first. If you cannot hold it that long, then end the interval, recover, and try again for a little longer period of time. Ride easily for 3 minutes between intervals. Work your way up to 4 x 5-minute intervals. Total workout length: 45 minutes.

Modifications: These intervals can also be done in combination with another workout, such as during a recovery ride or before you begin other intervals on your trainer. You can just throw 1 or 2 into your ride from time to time while out on rides, including endurance rides.

Chapter 10
Cross-Training Workouts

Specificity is a term that means that the best way to train for a given sport is to actually do that sport. So for cycling, the best training is to ride your bike. I have no argument with that. However, there are reasons why doing a different activity can be good for your cycling. First, if all you do is cycling, you'll become a one-dimensional athlete. You won't work some parts of your body or develop strength or fitness in areas other than those affected by cycling. Second, no matter how passionate you are about cycling, after a while it's a good mental break to do something different to add variety through a new and different challenge. Third, at the end of a long cycling season, it's good to give your body a break from riding and have it do a different activity. Also, during the winter when the weather isn't conducive to cycling outside and you dread riding your indoor trainer, get out and enjoy a winter sport. These can be very challenging and provide great strength and aerobic conditioning. Finally, there may be times such as when traveling or on vacation when you cannot cycle but there are other options available to you, such as using an elliptical machine, that you can use to maintain some of your cycling fitness. Cross-training means you are exercising in a manner different from cycling, such as skating or skiing. The cross-training workouts in this chapter have all been selected because they are very complementary to cycling in that they use somewhat similar muscles and are very aerobic in nature. Try these when you want or need a break from cycling and during your off-season. You may even discover a new sport to pursue.

Workout 78: Mountain Biking

Purpose of Workout: Although mountain biking is still riding a bike, it is a great way to ride in a very different atmosphere. When you are riding and training on the road all the time, no matter how much you love it, it can get a little old after a while, especially if you are doing a lot of structured training rides. Mountain biking allows you to get a good workout in for your legs and your heart but gives your head a break. I tend to view mountain biking as play. It's such a different way to ride a bike, especially when going off-road on single track, that you almost forget you are training. I don't have a computer on my mountain bike and just ride it for fun and cross-training, but I know I get my heart rate up pretty high. In addition, mountain biking adds the element of bike handling that is hard to get from road riding, unless you slide around corners on sand a lot. On single track, you are continually shifting your weight, riding through off-camber corners, balancing at near standstills, and sliding around corners. This helps train your responses to deal with these sensations, and these carry over to your road riding.

Course Description: You can mountain bike almost anywhere, and it's recommended to ride off-road. Choose single-track trails if you have them available or just ride on a gravel trail or dirt road. Use this opportunity to ride places you wouldn't go on your road bike.

Workout Description: Take off on your mountain bike and let the course dictate your tempo and effort. If riding single track, try to maintain a constant speed, avoid excessive braking, and try to be smooth going around trees and curves. Practice putting your foot out and sliding around tight bends. Learn to jump over small objects. Have fun. Total workout length: 1–2 hours.

Modifications: You can do many of the road workouts in this book on your mountain bike.

Workout 79: Ice Skating

Purpose of Workout: Ice skating is very complementary to cycling. The skating motion is a little different from cycling. You are pushing out to the side with skating as opposed to down with cycling, but you use the same main muscle groups (quads and buttocks). If done properly, this can be a leg strengthening and cardio workout. You also work your core very well in skating because you are balancing your weight over each foot and bending over. Plus, ice skating is much more fun than riding when it is 20 degrees (F) outside.

Course Description: This workout can be done either at an indoor or outdoor rink, or on a pond. If using a rink, be mindful of other people, who may make it challenging to get in a nice, steady workout. Also, if using speed skates, you need to be especially careful not to skewer others around you. If on an outdoor pond, of course you need to make sure the ice is solid enough everywhere on the pond, and you shouldn't skate alone.

Workout Description: Put your skates on and just start skating. If you don't know how, get some lessons and then just practice. Practice pushing forcefully straight out to the side and bending way down on your weighted leg, as if in a squat. Once you have your skating legs under you, try to maintain a steady pace for 5 minutes at a time, then skate gently for a few minutes, and repeat. If your ankles get tired, a brief rest sitting down will give your ankles a break, and you should be able to go again for several minutes. As you get more competent on your skates, you can even try doing intervals such as 1 lap on, 1 lap off around a rink. Total workout length: 60–90 minutes.

Modifications: If so inclined, you can play hockey for your workout. Or if you have a speed-skating club nearby, consider joining it for an alternate sport and competition in the winter. You can do short-track speed-skating races in a hockey rink and long-track events on outdoor tracks. Find more information at www.usspeedskating.org.

Workout 80: Inline Skating

__Purpose of Workout:__ Inline skating (Rollerblading®) is a very complementary activity to cycling. The skating motion is a little different from cycling. You are pushing out to the side with skating as opposed to pushing down with cycling, but you use the same main muscle groups (quads and buttocks). If done properly, this can be a leg strengthening and cardio workout. You also work your core very well in skating because you are balancing your weight over each foot and bending over. Plus, inline skating is a different activity and gives your mind a break from the cycling routine.

__Course Description:__ Inline skating can be done on any road or bike trail. You need to ensure the pavement is relatively smooth and free of cracks and bumps. It also needs to be clean of debris. On trails where there are joggers, walkers, and cyclists, you need to be aware of others around you. Be sure you can handle the hills that are on the course, especially the downhills. You can also look for indoor roller skating rinks. Some communities even have inline skating clubs and have weekly skating sessions scheduled, or you can just go to an open skating session and use your inline skates.

__Workout Description:__ Put your skates on and just start skating. If you don't know how, get some lessons and then just practice. Practice pushing straight out to the side and bending way down on your weighted leg, as if in a squat. Once you have your skating legs under you, try to maintain a steady pace for 5 minutes at a time, then skate gently for a few minutes and repeat. If your ankles get tired, a brief rest sitting down will give your ankles a break, and you should be able to go again for several minutes. As you get more competent on your skates, you can even try doing intervals such as 1 lap on, 1 lap off around a rink. Total workout length: 60–90 minutes.

__Modifications:__ If you have an inline skating club nearby, either indoor or outdoor, consider joining it for an alternate sport and training. Check out USA Rollersports at www.rollersports.usoc.org.

Workout 81: Hiking

Purpose of Workout: Hiking is a great activity that gives your body a different type of workout from what it's used to and also gives you a break mentally. Hiking out in nature is good for the body and soul, getting you away from traffic and people for a while. Hiking also gives you a decent cardiovascular workout. If the weather is cold or snowy and you can't get out for a long ride, a long hike can substitute. Add in some hills or climb a mountain and you get a serious leg workout as well as a cardio workout.

Course Description: You can hike anywhere there is a trail or road, or even cross-country through the woods blazing your own trail. You can follow a recreational trail, a hiking trail, or even a mountain bike single-track trail. If the trail is hilly or goes up a mountain, then it's all the better.

Workout Description: Good fitting hiking shoes are recommended for ankle support and to prevent blistering. Head out on the trail and hike. You can push the pace if you want more of a cardio workout. You should be able to get to and maintain a zone 2 (endurance pace) heart rate while hiking. As you get to hills, take smaller steps and keep your cadence up, similar to riding your bike. If going up a mountain, take it easy coming down as the eccentric motion of slowing yourself down with each foot strike will create soreness the next day, as your cycling legs are not used to this. Total workout length: 1–4 hours.

Modifications: Consider hiking with hiking poles to add some upper body motion and power to your hiking.

Workout 82: Hill Running

Purpose of Workout: Jogging and running aren't listed as one of these 101 workouts because they are quite a different activity from cycling, and too much running may be detrimental to your cycling training. However, running is a good cardiovascular workout and is convenient to do, especially when traveling. But here is a way to run that is more similar to cycling: running up hills. Hill running is more similar to the cycling motion and uses similar leg muscles while giving you a great cardiovascular workout, so it's listed here.

Course Description: You can run hills on roads, sidewalks, trails, or grassy fields. Just be sure it is smooth enough that you don't twist an ankle. Almost any hill will do, from short to long, gradual to steep.

Workout Description: Before running hills, be sure you have done a few runs on level surfaces to get your legs used to the running motion. You really don't want to jump right in to hill running without some running background. Warm up by running slowly for 10–15 minutes. As you get to your hill, accelerate up the hill, focusing on pushing off powerfully with your feet and turning your feet over rapidly. Pace yourself according to the length and steepness of the hill, but you should have no problem getting into your anaerobic (zone 5) range. Each hill interval should take from 1 to 2 minutes to complete. Walk or jog easily down the hill and repeat up to 10 times. Total workout length: 30–45 minutes.

Modification: If you don't have a hill available but have a multi-story building or stadium steps available, you can run stairs. See Workout 83.

Workout 83: Stair Climbing

Purpose of Workout: Running stairs is another fabulous and difficult workout when you don't have your bike. Stairs are often available when you travel, such as in multi-story hotels. It's a great cardiovascular workout that can easily be used for anaerobic interval workouts and is convenient to do, especially when traveling. Running up stairs is similar to the cycling motion and uses similar leg muscles while giving you a great cardiovascular workout.

Course Description: Find a staircase you can use that preferably has at least 5 stories. If it has fewer, you can still use it, but your intervals will be short and you'll need to do more of them. Another option is to run stairs at a stadium. These are usually high enough to give you a good 20–30-second interval.

Workout Description: Before running stairs, be sure you have done some running on level surfaces to get your legs used to the running motion. You really don't want to jump right in to stair running without some running background. Warm up by running slowly for 10–15 minutes. As you begin your stair run, you have to decide whether to run up every step or do them 2 at a time. Running every step requires faster leg turnover simulating spinning, while running up 2 steps at a time is similar to pushing a larger gear and will work more on your leg strength. You can use the railings to help pull yourself up or rely strictly on your legs. Run up the stairs at a fast, sustainable pace. The more flights you have, the more you have to manage your pace or you will quickly go anaerobic and be reduced to walking. Jog back down the stairs to recover (don't use the elevator) and repeat. Depending on the number of flights, you can do 10 or more intervals. Warm down by jogging or walking at the end. Total workout length: 30–45 minutes.

Modifications: If you look around, you may be able to find some stair climbing competitions near you. Many of these are charity fund-raisers and are a great workout as well as very unique events to add to your competitive résumé. Check out www.stairclimbingsports.com or the Yahoo Stairclimbing group.

Workout 84: Stair-Climbing Machine

Purpose of Workout: When forced to exercise indoors either due to weather or travel, one option is to hop on a stair-climbing machine at a fitness center or your home gym. Climbing stairs works the legs and also gives you a good cardio workout if you work hard enough.

Equipment: There are a couple of types of stair climbers. One type has 2 foot pads that go up and down and has varying speeds and/or resistances. The other type is often called a stepmill and has a moving set of stairs.

Workout Description: Warm up on the stair climber for 10 minutes in a moderately easy setting. Once warmed up, increase the resistance/speed of the machine to the desired level. You can do all sorts of intervals on these as you would on your bike, but due to the indoor nature, I'd recommend keeping these short and making it a threshold (zone 4) or anaerobic (zone 5) type of interval session. Try to get in 20–30 minutes at target effort, with rest periods between each interval. Warm down for 5 minutes. Wear your heart rate monitor to check your effort level. Total workout length: 35–45 minutes.

Exercise Description: There are some things to keep in mind when using a stair-climbing machine. 1) Stand upright and avoid bending over on the machine. 2) Avoid resting on your hands, elbows, or forearms. Use your hands as little as possible and only for balance; do not apply any more pressure on the handles than absolutely necessary. 3) Do not allow the steps to hit their top or bottom end of range. 4) By increasing the speed, the steps become shorter and your cadence increases, similar to shifting to a lower gear and spinning faster.

Workout 85: Elliptical Machine

Purpose of Workout: When forced to exercise indoors either due to weather or travel, another option is to hop on an elliptical machine at a fitness center or your home gym. Elliptical machines work the legs and also give you a good cardio workout if you work hard enough. Some machines have moving handles so you can get some upper body exercise at the same time, which helps to get your heart rate up even higher.

Equipment: Elliptical machines are all fairly similar. They have 2 foot pads that move in an elliptical, or oval, pattern, hence the name. Some machines have an adjustable stride length option available. If so, find a stride length that matches your stride.

Workout Description: Warm up on the elliptical machine for 10 minutes in a moderately easy setting. Once warmed up, increase the resistance/speed of the machine to the desired level. You can do all sorts of intervals on these as you would on your bike, but due to the indoor nature, I'd recommend keeping these short and making it a threshold (zone 4) or anaerobic (zone 5) type of interval session. Try to get in 20–30 minutes at target effort, with rest periods between each interval. Warm down for 5 minutes. Wear your heart rate monitor to check your effort level. Total workout length: 35–45 minutes.

Exercise Description: You can either move your feet in a forward pattern (feet go clockwise when viewed from the right), which is similar to walking uphill, or you can move them in a backwards pattern (feet go counterclockwise when viewed from the right side), which would mimic walking backwards down a hill. Either way is fine; it just gives you 2 different motion options. The forward motion is more similar to the cycling leg pattern though. You can hold on to the stationary handles or use the moving handles. The stationary handles give more support if you choose to do a vigorous workout, while the moving handles give your upper body some exercise and require more balance. Maintain an upright posture while on an elliptical machine; avoid bending over at the waist. You can increase the resistance of these machines, which creates a stress similar to riding up a hill. This applies more force to the legs and creates a greater leg strengthening workout.

Workout 86: Cross-Country Ski Machine

Purpose of Workout: When forced to exercise indoors either due to weather or travel, another option is to use a cross-country ski machine (such as Nordic Track®) at a fitness center or your home gym. Cross-country ski machines work the legs and arms, and also give you a great cardio workout. You will likely notice a higher heart rate for a given effort compared to cycling, because you are balancing and your arms are moving as well as your legs, so you are incorporating more muscle groups. You can get a very good leg and cardio workout on a cross-country ski machine and give yourself a break from the bike as well.

Equipment: Cross-country ski machines have 2 skis that move back and forth. There is adjustable resistance, so the leg action can be made more difficult. In place of ski poles, there are 2 handles attached to a cable that allows the hands to move back and forth as if you had ski poles. The hand cables also have adjustable resistance.

Workout Description: Warm up on the ski machine for 10 minutes in a moderately easy setting. Once warmed up, increase the resistance/speed of the machine to the desired level. You can do all sorts of intervals on these as you would on your bike, but due to the indoor nature, I'd recommend keeping these short and making it a threshold (zone 4) or anaerobic (zone 5) type of interval session. Try to get in 20–30 minutes at target effort, with rest periods between each interval. Warm down for 5 minutes. Wear your heart rate monitor to check your effort level. Total workout length: 35–45 minutes.

Exercise Description: You move your feet in a forward and backward pattern similar to the diagonal or classical stride of cross-country skiing. You hold onto the hand grips attached to the cables to mimic the arm motion with poles. Your arms work in an alternate fashion with your legs. When your left leg moves back, your left arm comes forward. Select a resistance that allows you to forcibly push back on the ski with each leg. Maintain an upright posture while on a cross-country ski machine; keep your hips pressed against the pad. You can increase the resistance to mimic going up hills to work your legs harder. You will find this works your lower back and is a good core strengthening exercise.

Workout 87: Cross-Country Skiing— Classic Stride

Purpose of Workout: Cross-country skiing is a very complementary activity to cycling. The classic or diagonal stride is the traditional cross-country skiing stride, where you skate in 2 tracks and you kick back with your skis to propel yourself forward. This is a similar motion to the cycling pedal stroke, and you also pull up and forward with the foot after the kick. You also work your core very well, especially your lower back, in cross-country skiing. And cross-country skiing is well known for giving an extremely good cardio workout. Your heart rate will get very high because you are using so many muscles in your body all at the same time.

Course Description: Obviously you need snow to do cross-country skiing, at least a good 6-inch base. You don't need groomed trails, but they make it much more enjoyable and allow you to glide along fast. If you don't have any groomed trails nearby, go make your own set of trails. You will probably want to make a loop so that you can go over it several times—the more you go over your tracks, the better packed they get and allow you to push off with more force. If you aren't careful, you'll be exhausted by the time you finally get your track well developed. Or, you can just head out and blaze a trail all day. Either way, you get a great workout. If you have groomed trails, just head out on them and explore.

Workout Description: Waxless skis are recommended if you are new to cross-country skiing because waxing skis is an art and you can get really frustrated trying to learn it by trial and error. If you don't know how to ski, take some lessons and then practice. At first, just cruise around getting the feel for kicking off with your feet powerfully and balancing on one foot as you glide between kicks. After you get the hang of it, try pushing your pace for a few minutes at a time, then backing off and recovering. Any hill you come to will undoubtedly increase your heart rate to zone 4 or 5. You will get a good workout in regardless of how hard you push. Try skiing without poles to help improve your balance. Total workout length: 60–90 minutes.

Modifications: If you live in an area with a lot of snow, consider ski racing during the winter. It will give you as good, or even better, cardiovascular fitness as from cycling, and it will give you a different competitive outlet during your cycling off-season. Check out the US Ski and Snowboard Association at www.ussa.org for more information.

Workout 88: Cross-Country Skiing— Skate Stride

Purpose of Workout: Cross-country skiing is a very complementary activity to cycling. The free technique or skate stride is a newer cross-country skiing technique, where you skate on a smooth groomed trail and you push to the sides with your feet, a motion similar to ice skating. That's why it's called "skate" skiing. This uses muscles similar to those used in the cycling pedal stroke, so it's good cross-training. You also work your core very well, especially your lower back, in cross-country skiing. Cross-country skate skiing is famous for giving an extremely good cardio workout. Your heart rate will get very high because you are using so many muscles in your body all at the same time.

Course Description: You really need trails groomed for skate skiing if you plan to do it, which means you'll need to go to a resort or facility that offers it. Trails will vary in difficultly and are usually marked accordingly, similar to downhill runs.

Workout Description: Lessons are highly recommended when first starting. There is a lot of technique involved. At first, just cruise around learning to push off with your feet powerfully and balancing on one foot as you glide between kicks. After you get the hang of it, try pushing your pace for a few minutes at a time, then backing off and recovering. You will get a good workout in regardless of how hard you push. As you get more accomplished, you can work on hills that are sure to give you a great cardio workout. Total workout length: 60–90 minutes.

Modifications: If you live in an area with a lot of snow, consider ski racing during the winter. It will give you as good, or even better, cardiovascular fitness as from cycling, and it will give you a different competitive outlet during your cycling off-season. Check out the US Ski and Snowboard Association at www.ussa.org for more information.

Workout 89: Snowshoeing

Purpose of Workout: Snowshoeing is another great winter exercise that will use your leg muscles while also giving you a terrific cardio workout. Your legs work hard because they are lifting the snowshoes against the resistance and depth of the snow. The deeper the snow, the greater the resistance. Your heart rate will get very high because you are using so many muscles in your body all at the same time. You can adjust your pace from walking (or trudging if the snow is really deep) to running to get the level of cardio workout you want. Regardless of how fast or slow you go, you are sure to get a good cardio workout. This is a great substitute for a long easy ride in the winter.

Course Description: Obviously you need snow to snowshoe, at least a few inches. You don't need prepared trails—you can make your own. If you are on a snowshoe trail, you will find it easier because the loose snow has been trampled down, allowing you to walk or run more easily. Just head out in the snow and blaze your own trail if you need to. Just doing that constitutes a great workout. Or, you can make a loop and develop a trail on which you can do laps. Include some hills to add to the leg work and cardio effort required.

Workout Description: If snowshoeing for the first time, just walk around getting the feel for walking with snowshoes and balancing. After you get the hang of it, try pushing your pace higher for a few minutes at a time, then backing off and recovering. You will get a good workout in regardless of how hard you push. You can snowshoe with ski poles if you want some assistance with balancing and also to get some upper body exercise. Total workout length: 60–90 minutes.

Modifications: If you live in an area with a snowshoe club, consider snowshoe racing during the winter. It will give you as good, or even better, cardiovascular fitness as from cycling, and it will give you a different competitive outlet during your cycling off-season. Check out the US Snowshoe Association at www.snowshoeracing.com for more information.

Chapter 11
Testing Workouts

As you become more experienced and competitive, you may wish to know how fit you have become, either compared to yourself or compared to others. Testing is a way to obtain information about your relative fitness. Included in this chapter are a number of tests that you can conduct by yourself, without a lot of fancy and expensive lab equipment. By doing these periodically throughout the season and off-season, you can gauge how fit you are—or how unfit you may have become over the winter. If you do these, keep a log and write down the date and your results so you can compare the results with future tests and track your progress. If you are testing yourself and want an accurate result, make sure you are fully rested before attempting these. Give yourself at least 2 recovery days before you do these tests. But there is also another reason for doing these—these tests are also great workouts. They are strenuous but short efforts, so if you don't have a lot of time but want a good workout, consider one of these.

Workout 90: Ramp Test with Power Meter

Purpose of Workout: This workout is a test to determine your current power-generating ability. This test is useful to track your power throughout the year. The resulting wattage number itself doesn't mean much but becomes informative once you've done 2 or 3 of these tests and have developed a baseline. It is able to tell you whether you are becoming more powerful or not compared to past tests. It's good to do 1 of these tests at the beginning of your off-season, 2 or 3 during your off-season, and then about every 4 weeks during the season. Although this is a test, it is also a great workout in and of itself. This test is extremely difficult and should only be done if you are fit and healthy. You will exceed your anaerobic threshold heart rate.

Course Description: This test is done with a power meter such as PowerTap® or SRM® on your bike. It can also be done on a trainer that has power measurement capability such as CompuTrainer®. Ideally this workout is done indoors on a trainer, in a very controlled and repeatable environment so as to allow you to focus on reaching and holding the desired wattage. This can be done outside if you have a very level road with little traffic or a closed course. However, outside wind and any hills will make it quite difficult to hold your desired wattage, especially when you reach the end and are very tired. Also, the outside conditions vary from test to test, making it more challenging to compare results.

Workout Description: Start out by warming up very thoroughly, at least 15 minutes, including some short hard efforts. Begin the test at a fairly low wattage. This should be about 100 watts below your threshold level. If you do not know your threshold, then start at 150 watts. Hold the starting wattage for 2 minutes, trying to be as steady as possible and keeping your power within a few watts of the target. After the first 2 minutes, increase your wattage by 20 watts. Hold this wattage for 2 more minutes. Continue to increase your effort and wattage by 20 watts every 2 minutes until you can no longer hold that effort. At this point, the test is over. Warm down for 10 minutes. Record your wattage and time in the last interval, along with your heart rate, and compare it with previous results and keep it for future reference. Total workout length: less than 1 hour.

Modifications: You can vary the duration of each step, such as holding for 3 minutes versus 2 minutes. Keep in mind that if you make them longer, your wattage won't be as high by the time you reach exhaustion as it would be with shorter steps. The main thing to remember is to always use the same protocol so you can compare your results from test to test. If you do not have a power meter on your bike, see Workout 91.

Workout 91: Ramp Test without Power Meter

Purpose of Workout: This workout is a test to determine the current fitness level for those without a power meter. This test is useful to track your fitness throughout the year. You will use your gears and trainer resistance to determine your relative fitness. If you have a heart rate monitor and cadence meter, those are helpful to use as well. It's good to do 1 of these at your peak fitness in the middle to the end of the season, 1 at the beginning of your off-season, 2 or 3 during your off-season, and then about every 4 weeks during the season. Although this is a test, it is also a great workout in and of itself. This test is extremely difficult and should only be done if you are very fit and healthy. You will exceed your anaerobic threshold heart rate.

Course Description: This test is done with your bike mounted on an indoor trainer that has variable resistance settings. This workout really isn't designed to do outside, as the vagaries of wind and changes in elevation make it very difficult to maintain the constant pace required for this test. You will use your gears to incrementally increase the resistance throughout the test.

Workout Description: Start out by warming up very thoroughly, at least 15 minutes. Start the test by using your large chainring in the front and one of your largest cogs on the back wheel. This will give you plenty of gears to use during the test. You should start out below your threshold level effort. Begin the test by selecting a resistance setting on your trainer that allows you to ride at a moderately hard intensity in the initial gear you have chosen. Hold the starting pace and gear for 2 minutes, and keeping your cadence as steady as possible. Your target cadence should ideally be between 85 and 100 RPM. After the first 2 minutes, increase to your next larger gear (next smaller cog in the back) while maintaining the same cadence. Hold this gear and cadence for 2 more minutes. Continue to increase your gear by shifting to your next smaller cog every 2 minutes until you can no longer hold your effort or cadence. At this point, the test is over. Cool down for 10 minutes. Record your gear and time in the last interval, along with your heart rate, and compare it with previous results and keep it for future reference. For example, perhaps you were able to hold your 53 x 15 gear for 1 minute and 35 seconds. Next time, see if you can hold it for 2 minutes or make it to the 53 x 14 gear. Total workout length: less than 1 hour.

Modifications: You can vary the duration of each step, such as holding each step for 3 minutes instead of 2 minutes. Keep in mind that if you make each step longer, you won't be able to reach as high a gear by the time you reach exhaustion as you would with shorter steps. The main thing to remember is to always use the same protocol so you can compare your results from test to test. If you have a power meter on your bike, see Workout 90.

Workout 92: 6-Minute Power Test

Purpose of Workout: This workout is a test to determine your current power-generating ability using a 6-minute test. This test is useful to track your power throughout the year. The resulting wattage number is useful as a reference point for planning the intensity of your workouts. The result of this power test is the maximum amount of power you can generate and hold during a 6-minute effort. By knowing this value, you can judge the amount of power you should target for shorter and longer intervals. For example, if your average power from this 6-minute test is 300 watts, then you should be able to generate more wattage for a 3-minute interval and slightly less for a 10-minute interval. This test can also be used to track your progress throughout the season to tell you whether you are becoming fitter or not compared to past tests. It's good to do one of these tests every 4 weeks during the season and at least once during the off-season. Although this is a test, it is also a tough workout in and of itself, both physically and mentally. This test is extremely difficult and should only be done if you are very fit and healthy. You will exceed your anaerobic threshold heart rate.

Course Description: This test is done with a power meter such as PowerTap® or SRM® on your bike. It can also be done on a trainer that has power measurement capability such as CompuTrainer®. This workout can be done indoors, in a very controlled environment so as to allow you to focus on reaching and holding the desired pace. This can be done outside if you have a very level road with little traffic or a closed course. However, if done outside, the wind and any hills will make it more difficult to maintain your pace.

Workout Description: Start out by warming up very thoroughly, at least 15 minutes, and include some short but intense efforts. Begin the test by riding at an effort you believe you can hold for 6 minutes. The first time you may be guessing and go out too fast or slow. Spin easily for 10 minutes and then repeat the 6-minute test. Warm down for 10 minutes. Record your wattage and time in each 6-minute test, along with your heart rate, and compare it with previous results and keep it for future reference. Total workout length: less than 1 hour.

Modifications: If you do not have a power meter on your bike, see Workout 93.

Workout 93: 20-Minute Threshold Test

Purpose of Workout: This workout is a test to determine your current aerobic fitness. It requires that you have a heart rate monitor and is especially good to do with a power meter if you have one. This test is useful to track your aerobic threshold throughout the year. It's good to do this test regularly throughout the season and even a couple times during the off-season. This test is long enough that you will be riding at or slightly above your threshold pace, where threshold pace is defined as the maximum pace you can hold for 1 hour. Knowing your threshold pace, in terms of either heart rate or power, is very informative. It can tell you the status of your aerobic fitness, which changes throughout the year and can be used to track progress during the season and from one season to the next. It is also required to determine your anaerobic threshold, which is used to determine your various training zones, 1 through 6, which are used throughout this book. Although this is a test, it is also a great workout in and of itself.

Course Description: This test is done on an indoor trainer such as CompuTrainer, on rollers with resistance, or outside if you have a very level road with little traffic or a closed course. However, if done outside, wind and any hills will make it more difficult to maintain your pace. Conducting the test indoors will result in a more repeatable result from test to test.

Workout Description: Start out by warming up very thoroughly, at least 15 minutes. Start your 20-minute time trial and record your heart rate and power if you have that capability. Concentrate on pushing yourself to ride as hard as you can for the 20 minutes. Pacing is critical. It's very easy to start out too fast and not be able to hold that pace for the full 20 minutes. You will likely have to do this test 2 or 3 times before you determine your sustainable pace and heart rate. If you finish with a burst at the end, then you didn't go hard enough during the 20 minutes. Warm down for 10 minutes. Record your average heart rate as well as power if you have it. Compare it with previous results and keep it for future reference. Your threshold pace for 1 hour is about

95% of the value you obtain from this test. That's because you can go slightly anaerobic during a 20-minute test, which you wouldn't be able to do for a full hour. Total workout length: 1 hour.

Modification: You can use a short time trial as a threshold test as well (Workout 94). If you have a short time trial in the range from 12 to 20 km, it can serve as a good threshold test. Just keep in mind that in a real race, you will be more psyched and able to put in a greater effort and will probably be more anaerobic, which will result in a higher heart rate or power average.

Chapter 12
Races as Workouts

While races are often the reason for training, races are also great training workouts. Races are the most intense workouts you will do. You will push yourself harder than you do in training; therefore, you will push yourself to a new level of fitness as well. You may have heard the expression "racing into shape." This implies that if you race often, you will work yourself into great shape, which is true. However, "racing into shape" is difficult on both the body and morale. If you go into a race when you are not in great shape and want to use it for training, you will be worked over by those who are in shape and will likely be dropped. But a local early season training race series that is low-key and does not offer much in the way of prizes is ideal for using as training. It doesn't matter if you get dropped or don't place—what matters is whether you get a fantastic workout. Listed in this chapter are the main types of races you will likely find that you can use for training. One word of caution: if you are new to racing and are using races as training, be sure you have the skills necessary to ride with experienced racers. If not, it's best to find a team with which to train first to learn those skills.

Workout 94: Time Trials

Purpose of Workout: A time trial is a great test of your fitness. You are likely going to be more prepared physically and more psyched mentally going into a race than into a training session, so you will likely get your true maximal effort and set a personal best time. If your time trial is part of a series or a race you do every year, you can do some comparison from year to year, although don't depend entirely on this as the environmental conditions from race to race will vary and have significant impacts on your time. A slight difference in breeze, even as low as 5 MPH, can really change your speed. If you have a power meter, that provides a more repeatable measure of effort than heart rate or speed during a time trial.

Course Description: The course is determined by the race organizer. Typically time trial courses are as flat as possible, but sometimes hills are present, either out of necessity or because the race organizer chose to include them. Most racers like to race on a flat course to try to set personal bests for the distance, so organizers typically seek out as flat a course as possible with few turns. They are usually an out-and-back course with one 180 degree turnaround at the far end.

Workout Description: Start out by warming up very thoroughly, at least for 30 minutes. If it is a shorter time trial, you will actually want to warm up longer than the duration of the race, as you will be putting out an intense effort. Warm up right up to your start time. Some prefer to warm up on a trainer while others prefer warming up on the road. In either case, keep an eye on the start line and make sure you don't miss your start. Check the start list and see the names and numbers of the 3 riders starting before you as well as the estimated start time. Check frequently to see who is starting. You don't want to miss your start. The clock starts whether you are there or not. Come to the start line sweating and with your heart rate elevated and try not to stand around any longer than possible. Start the race by controlling your speed, power, and/or heart rate. The natural tendency is to start out too quickly and go anaerobic, which hurts your overall time. Once you've gone anaerobic, it's difficult to recover because you will be pushing at your anaerobic threshold throughout the event. Concentrate on moving your feet in smooth circles with every pedal stroke. You'll need to pace your effort for the distance, so that you don't tire before the end, but so that you do use all your energy up by the end. You should finish exhausted and not have any energy left to sprint. Spin easily for 10 minutes after the race. Record your race data (speed, time, heart rate, and/or power) and compare to similar race distances. If these are short races, such as 12–20 km, you can use this information to determine your aerobic threshold. In a short race, your heart rate and power will be towards the high end of zone 4.

Workout 95: Road Races

Purpose of Workout: If you are training as a road cyclist, there's no better way to get a great workout than by entering a road race, with one exception. If you are not prepared and don't have enough fitness to stay with the pack, you will get dropped and end up doing a training ride by yourself. If that's the case, you might as well stay home and ride by yourself or with others of similar ability. But if you can hang with a pack at least for a good portion of the race, you will work harder than you can in a training ride. There's just something about the competition and the fear of being dropped in a race that forces one to push as hard as possible.

Course Description: The course is determined by the race organizer. Road races can vary considerably as to type of course. Some are absolutely flat but may be windy; others are ruthlessly hilly; and others add just a mixture of hills. Some courses are short and several laps are ridden (circuit race), and some are long single-loop courses or point-to-point races. Road races are the longest of all races with distances of more than 100 miles common.

Workout Description: Start out by warming up. Depending on the nature of the race, some road races start out at a mellow pace and build up speed. But don't assume that will be the case; be ready to ride fast from the gun. If you are weaker than many of the competitors, your goal may simply be to finish with the pack or stay with it as long as possible. You can still get a great workout trying to stay with the pack if you are weaker than the other riders. If you are fitter than most in the race, use the race as a test of yourself and your tactics by attacking and trying to break away, multiple times if necessary. If the race result isn't necessarily that important to you, treat the race as a training ride and take some chances. You never know, you may just succeed in breaking away and staying away.

Modification: Training race series are especially good for this sort of workout, as the name implies. These are often low-key events with not much on the line in the way of prizes, so they are good opportunities to go out and try some things that you wouldn't necessarily try during an important race.

Workout 96: Criteriums

Purpose of Workout: Criteriums, those fast races around a short course with lots of corners, are another super way to get in a very hard workout. They are also good events to practice your pack riding skill; just make sure you are ready so as not to be a hazard to the other riders.

Course Description: The course is determined by the race organizer. Standard criteriums are usually ½ to ¾ mile long (about a kilometer) and have 4 to 6 corners. Some are longer and more like a circuit race. They may have some very sharp corners or downhill corners requiring good bike-handling skill, especially when raced in the rain. Some have short but steep hills to make it more interesting and challenging.

Workout Description: Start out by warming up. Criteriums almost always start fast, so be very well warmed up and ready for a hard effort right from the gun. If you aren't as strong as your fellow competitors, you will work hard just trying to stay with the pack and work on your bike-handling and pack-riding skills. If you are more competitive, you can practice your riding skills by cornering without braking, moving around in the pack, and even trying to break away. If the race result isn't necessarily that important to you, treat the race as a training ride and take some chances. You never know, you may just succeed in breaking away and staying away. Or, go for primes if they are offered and of course work on setting up your sprint at the end.

Modification: Training race series are especially good for this sort of workout, as the name implies. These are often low-key events with not much on the line in the way of prizes, so they are good opportunities to go out and try some things that you wouldn't necessarily try during an important race.

Workout 97: Mountain Bike Races

Purpose of Workout: If you consider yourself primarily a road cyclist, there's nothing like a mountain bike race to humble you. Mountain bike racing not only requires a high level of aerobic and anaerobic fitness and hill-climbing ability; it also requires very good balance and bike-handling skills. There also isn't any type of racing that's more exciting and exhausting, yet it's also a blast and a great diversion from riding the roads all the time. If you are a road cyclist who races many weekends a year on pavement, hit the trails and compete on a mountain bike for a nice refresher. Treat these as fun races and don't worry about how you place; just use them as intense training rides. Plus you'll meet an entirely different segment of the cycle racing population and get to race in some very nice places.

Course Description: The course is determined by the race organizer. It will most likely have a majority as single track and some as double track or dirt roads. Although called "mountain" bike races, unless you live in the mountains, these are more likely just very hilly races off-road. Race promoters usually go out of their way to find steep, challenging hills and have you do them several times. The course will likely go through stream crossings and mud, and over logs and rocks.

Workout Description: Start out by warming up. Unless the course is more than 5 miles, you should get there early enough to ride the entire course for your warm-up as this will help you navigate the course at race speed. Mountain bike races start out extremely fast as everyone is trying to get to the front of the pack before it hits the single track. Be prepared and thoroughly warmed up at the start and be ready to sprint right from the start. It's kind of backwards from road races where the sprint is at the end. The first lap may be very fast if you can get a position towards the front, or it may actually be the slowest if you get behind slower riders in the single-track sections. Practice holding your speed through corners as much as possible while using your brakes only when necessary. Try to catch riders in front or stay with those who pass you. I view mountain bike races as a combination of a time trial and criterium. Due to the technical nature of mountain bike courses, you are slowing and accelerating all the time just like in a criterium, which is good for speed, power, and anaerobic fitness. Once the race gets spread out, you may very well be riding by yourself to the end, similar to time trialing, except for the steep hills that are often present in mountain bike races. As you can see, you can train many aspects of your fitness in a mountain bike race. It also helps explain why mountain bike racers do well if they switch over to road racing—they are very fit and skilled cyclists.

Workout 98: Cyclocross Races

Purpose of Workout: Cyclocross racing is an entirely unique cycling discipline and sport, but it is great training for road cyclists. Cyclocross racing takes place in the fall and early winter and provides an opportunity to train hard and race well into the winter, allowing you the opportunity of maintaining or perhaps even improving your fitness late in the season, which will help translate into better fitness come spring. It also incorporates running, which road cyclists will find challenging and exhausting but really helps with the aerobic and anaerobic fitness. Finally, cyclocross is very technical, perhaps more so than mountain biking in terms of the terrain and obstacles you need to maneuver. You will need to ride through sand, mud, and perhaps snow; jump off and run over obstacles; and get back on without missing a beat.

Course Description: The course is determined by the race organizer. It will most likely have a combination of off-road sections on dirt roads or trails, across open fields, through water, and will likely have some pavement. There will most likely be hills to ride and/or run up. They will also include man-made obstacles such as barriers to jump over.

Workout Description: Start out by warming up. You should get to the race in time to ride the entire course a few times as this will help you navigate the course at race speed. Practice holding your speed through corners, over barriers, and through mud, sand, and water crossings. Try to catch riders in front or stay with those who pass you. Learn to pace yourself. These races are long enough that you won't be able to be anaerobic a lot of the time; you need to stay within your aerobic zone as much as possible. Due to the very technical nature of cyclocross courses, you are slowing and accelerating, and hopping off and on the bike, which is good for speed, power, and anaerobic fitness. The sustained duration of the races works on your aerobic fitness and endurance.

Chapter 13
Recovery Exercises

These exercises will help you recover after one of your other workouts. As mentioned in Chapter 2, recovery is just as important as training, as it's the recovery that makes you stronger. The faster you can recover, the sooner you can train hard again. This chapter discusses massage and stretching, techniques that can help your muscles recover more quickly. Also, don't forget proper nutrition. Refueling your body will allow you to recover more quickly as well. While nutrition is not covered in this book, there are a large number of books and resources that do cover athletic nutrition.

Workout 99: Self-Massage

Purpose of Workout: If you follow bike racing at all, you know that all the pro cyclists get massages every night. They use it to loosen tight muscles, reduce swelling, increase circulation, flush waste products from their leg muscles, and relax. Even without the benefit of having your own personal masseuse/masseur, you can massage your own legs and get much of the same benefit. Self-massage is a recovery technique, and you can do it as often as you wish, after every workout if you have the time. It's also a great way to just unwind and relax after a hard ride. Not only is a self-massage free, it also gives you immediate feedback on tight or sore areas.

Equipment: You can do a massage with only your hands, using massage oils to lubricate your skin. One of the common reasons given for men cyclists shaving their legs is so that it is easier to massage, especially when using oil, and for cleanup. So use massage oil to justify shaving your legs! You may also choose to use a massage stick.

Workout Description: Sitting on a chair, place your feet forward flat on the floor with your knees bent. Oil your legs and start the massage by cupping your hands and stroking firmly upwards from the ankle to the knee, working the calf muscles. Then work the front, outside, and back of the thighs by stroking from the knee to the hip. Use firmer strokes as you work up from the ankles to the hips. You may choose to make a fist and knead with your knuckles for your thighs. Stroke each muscle group at least 5 times with each hand. Next, knead your leg muscles by squeezing and releasing the muscles with each hand. You may then do some soft pounding on your muscles with the side of your hands or fists. Finish off with gentle strokes with your hands, over your entire legs.

Modification: Of course, if you have the resources and availability, you can hire someone to give you a massage. It may only be occasionally, but if you do, try to find one who has experience with athletes. There are a number of Web sites and books available that go into much more detail and can give you a lot of other ideas on how to do self-massage.

Workout 100: Stretching

Purpose of Workout: Stretching has a number of benefits for cyclists. The touted benefits include flexibility, or increased range of motion; injury prevention; and reduced muscle soreness. Flexibility is important for cyclists because flexible muscles and connective tissue facilitates the ability to generate and transmit power to the pedals while maintaining an aerodynamic position on the bike. This is especially important for time trialists in an aerodynamic position. Of particular importance to cyclists is hamstring and gluteal muscle flexibility. Stretching is also promoted as a way to avoid injury, and while cycling does not have the extended range or motion or abrupt impacts of other sports, stretching can still help avoid overuse injuries due to tight muscles and ligaments. Stretching may also aid recovery by flushing waste products out of the muscles, speeding recovery, and reducing delayed onset muscle soreness, although it is somewhat unclear whether stretching reduces muscle soreness. Stretching, like massage, is also helpful in that it allows you to relax both mind and body after a workout.

Stretching for cyclists is recommended *after* a workout rather than before. This is because the body tissues are warmed and most amenable to stretching. Stretching cold muscles, tendons, and ligaments prior to exercise may increase injury risk. If you feel tight and want to stretch prior to a ride, it's still best to warm up on the bike for 5–10 minutes before attempting stretching. Riding your bike during a warm-up is always an excellent way to warm up and loosen up your muscles.

Equipment: An exercise band or a stretching strap is helpful to assist with stretching.

Workout Description: There are different stretching techniques: static stretching, proprioceptive neuromuscular facilitation (PNF) stretching, active isolated stretching (AIS), ballistic stretching, and assisted stretching, to name a few. The one discussed here is static stretching, which is the easiest to do and most familiar to people. Static stretching involves holding the stretched position for 30 seconds. This involves relaxing and stretching the muscles simultaneously without any fast movement or bouncing. Stretch until you feel mild discomfort to your muscles. Do not stretch to pain. Hold this stretch for 30 seconds and think about relaxing your muscles as you stretch—you should be able to continue to stretch further as you relax. Don't forget to breathe as you are stretching. This will help with relaxation. Repeat the stretch with the opposite leg. You can do each stretch once or twice per session.

There is a lot of debate in fitness circles about which method of stretching is most effective. I believe that the fact that you do stretching on a regular basis is much more important than the specific technique you use. Below, basic cycling stretches are described to stretch the lower body.

Hamstring Stretch: Sit on the floor with one leg extended in front and the other with the knee bent and the foot up against the other knee. Do not bend the leg out as in the hurdler's stretch as this puts stress on the bent knee. Bend forward at the waist and reach toward the extended foot. However, *do not bend* the spine or round the shoulders. To maximize the stretch to the hamstrings, concentrate on bending at the waist. Think about trying to extend your navel toward your extended foot. You will feel the stretch to your hamstrings. Don't worry about whether you can touch your toes as long as you are feeling a stretch in the hamstrings. Hold for 30 seconds and repeat with the other leg. An alternative method is to stand holding your bike with one hand on the handlebar and the other hand on the saddle. Put one foot on the top tube and bend forward at the waist and hold for 30 seconds.

Calf Stretch: Stand with the hands on a wall with the feet shoulder-width apart, about 12 inches from the wall. Step back about 24 inches with one foot. While keeping the heel of the extended foot on the floor, bend towards the wall by bending your elbows and shifting your hips towards the wall until you feel a mild stretch. Hold this stretch for 30 seconds and then switch legs. You can also do this stretch with your bike. Place one hand on the handlebars and the other on the saddle, step back with one foot, and do the stretch as described above.

Glute Stretch: The starting position is on the floor on your hands and knees. Extend your right leg back with the knee and toes on the floor.

Bend the left leg up at the waist, lowering yourself to the floor. Bend your left knee in, so as to bring your left foot to the right so it is under your right hip. Bend forward at the waist and reach over your head. Try to bring your stomach down onto your left leg. You will feel a stretch in your left gluteal muscles. Hold for 30 seconds and repeat for the other side.

Quad Stretch: Stand on your left leg and bend the right knee and foot back. Grab your right foot with your left hand and pull it up and against your left buttock. Straighten out your right leg by pulling your knee back, and stand completely upright. You will feel a stretch in the front of your right quadriceps muscle. You may need to hold onto something with your free hand for balance. Hold for 30 seconds and then repeat with the other leg.

Modifications: If you are interested in learning more about different stretches and techniques, there are a number of books and online resources available that explain stretching in much more detail.

Chapter 14
Workout 101: The Joy Ride!

Purpose of Workout: If you have made it this far into this book, you ride a bike and most likely you started riding a bike as a kid for the pure joy of it. The bicycle was a toy. No matter how serious and structured your cycling riding and training has become, never forget why you took bicycling up in the first place—because IT'S FUN! This ride is intended to remind you why you ride bikes and to keep it fun. Do this workout at least once a month and whenever you feel like riding is becoming a burden. Riding your bike should be something you *want to do*, not something you *have to do*. If you ever start feeling that you *have* to ride your bike, pull out this workout for a day or two. It will remind you why you ride and why you should keep doing it. Because riding a bike is first and foremost *fun*!

Course Description: Your favorite course.

Workout Description: Put on your favorite jersey and socks, take off your bike computer and heart rate monitor, and go for a ride for the pure joy and fun of it. Go easily or push yourself—whatever you feel like. Pay attention to the ride (don't think about work for heaven's sake) and enjoy the scenery going by. Total workout length: as long or as short as you want.

Modification: Take a friend, spouse, or kids along with you. Stop and have a snack along the way.

About the Author

Coach David Ertl has been riding and racing bikes practically all his life. He began riding at the age of five, began competing in 1973, and continues to compete as a master's athlete to this day. David became a certified coach with USA Cycling in 2002. In 2004 he became a certified personal trainer with the National Strength and Conditioning Association (NSCA) and in 2007 obtained the highest coaching level offered by USA Cycling, Level 1. David coaches individual cyclists as well as two teams, the Des Moines Cycle Club Race Team and the Iowa Chapter of the JDRF Ride to Cure Diabetes Team. In addition to personal coaching, David also provides online training plans and information, including fifteen-week and annual training plans for recreational and competitive cyclists and triathletes. Learn more about his background and coaching programs at www.CyclesportCoaching.com.

He and his wife, Angie, own the 24/7 X-Press Fitness Center and Pilates Studio in Des Moines, Iowa. He and his family ride and reside in Waukee, Iowa.

He can be reached at Coach@CyclesportCoaching.com.

Special Thank You Bonus Offer for Purchasing
"101 Cycling Workouts"

Now that you have purchased "101 Cycling Workouts", here's your chance to put these workouts together into a logical, structured training plan for **free** as my Thank You for purchasing my book.

I am offering you a Training Plan Template to use in designing a year-round structured training plan using the workouts listed in "101 Cycling Workouts". This Training Plan Template allows you to select workouts from chapters in this book. This template indicates which type of workout to do each day, for 365 days of the year! Just select your desired workout from the appropriate chapter indicated in the plan and you will have yourself a systematic training plan. You can reuse this every year as well!

This training plan is worth $49 and it's yours absolutely free.

To download your free copy of the Training Plan Template,
you may either visit:

www.CyclesportCoaching.com/Bonus.html

or email me at:

Coach@CyclesportCoaching.com

BUY A SHARE OF THE FUTURE IN YOUR COMMUNITY

These certificates make great holiday, graduation and birthday gifts that can be personalized with the recipient's name. The cost of one S.H.A.R.E. or one square foot is $54.17. The personalized certificate is suitable for framing and will state the number of shares purchased and the amount of each share, as well as the recipient's name. The home that you participate in "building" will last for many years and will continue to grow in value.

Here is a sample SHARE certificate:

YES, I WOULD LIKE TO HELP!

*I support the work that Habitat for Humanity does and I want to be part of the excitement! As a donor, I will receive periodic updates on your construction activities but, more importantly, I know my gift will help a family in our community realize the dream of homeownership. **I would like to SHARE in your efforts against substandard housing in my community!** (Please print below)*

PLEASE SEND ME _____ SHARES at $54.17 EACH = $ $_____

In Honor Of: _____

Occasion: (Circle One)   HOLIDAY   BIRTHDAY   ANNIVERSARY

      OTHER: _____

Address of Recipient: _____

Gift From: _____ *Donor Address:* _____

Donor Email: _____

I AM ENCLOSING A CHECK FOR $ $_____ PAYABLE TO HABITAT FOR HUMANITY OR PLEASE CHARGE MY VISA OR MASTERCARD (CIRCLE ONE)

Card Number _____ Expiration Date: _____

Name as it appears on Credit Card _____ Charge Amount $ _____

Signature _____

Billing Address _____

Telephone # Day _____ Eve _____

PLEASE NOTE: Your contribution is tax-deductible to the fullest extent allowed by law.
Habitat for Humanity • P.O. Box 1443 • Newport News, VA 23601 • 757-596-5553
www.HelpHabitatforHumanity.org

Printed in the USA
CPSIA information can be obtained
at www.ICGtesting.com
JSHW012033140824
68134JS00033B/3036